Where Words Come From

Where Words Come From

A Dictionary of Word Origins

Fred Sedgwick

continuum

Continuum International Publishing Group

The Tower Building   80 Maiden Lane
11 York Road   Suite 704
London SE1 7NX   New York NY 10038

www.continuumbooks.com

British Library Cataloguing-in-Publication Data
A catalogue record for this book is available from the British Library.

ISBN: 978-1-8470-6274-1 (Paperback)

Library of Congress Cataloging-in-Publication Data
The Publisher has applied for CIP data.

Typeset by Newgen Imaging Systems Pvt Ltd, Chennai, India

For Cariad

North of Crimea
four thousand-odd years ago
they said (or something like it)
qha. And Germanic and Scandinavian
ale-and-potato men
took their 'whore' words from it,
hore, huora, hors.

But *qha* took journeys
south and west
and here is Latin *carus,*
caritas, Irish *caraim,* 'I love',
'caress'
and Welsh, *Cariad.*

Contents

Acknowledgements

Tony Allsworth, Terri Morgan, Colin Sedgwick, Henry Burns Eliot, Emily Roeves, Dorothy Hampson.

A List of Abbreviations

In this book foreign words are *italicized*.
The symbol > means that there is an entry under that word.

Amer. – American
Arab. – Arabic
A-S. – Anglo-Saxon
Aust. – Australia

Br. – British

Celt. – Celtic

Du. – Dutch

Eng. – English

f. – from [only when referring to the roots of words]
fem. – feminine
Fr. – French

Gael. – Gaelic
Ger. – German
Gk. – Greek
Guj. – Gujarati

Heb. – Hebrew

IE. – Indo-European
imit. – imitative
It. – Italian

L. – Latin
LG. – Low German

MD. – Middle Dutch
ME. – Middle English
MedL. – Medieval Latin

MLG. – Middle Low German
ModGer. – Modern German

NZ. – New Zealand

OE. – Old English
OFr. – Old French
OHG. – Old High German
OIce. Old Icelandic
OIr. – Old Irish
ON. – Old Norse
orig. – originally
OS. – Old Saxon

Pers. – Persian
Port. – Portuguese
prob. – probably

Rom – Romance

Sanskr. – Sanskrit
Scand. – Scandinavian
Sc. – Scots
Sp. – Spanish
Swed. – Swedish

ult. – ultimately
unc. orig. – uncertain origin
US. – as used in the United States / as an adjective
US – United States (as noun)

Yid. – Yiddish

Introduction

Mr Cooper was a Latin master at my London grammar school. We knew that *cupa* meant 'barrel' in the language he taught, so we called him that, rather like public schoolboys in the sort of school ours tried to emulate. One day he told us that the word 'sincere' came from two Latin words: *sine*, meaning 'without', and *cera*, meaning 'wax'. A jar on sale in the market might have been broken and glued together with wax. On the other hand, one that was still intact was *sine cera*. Hence our word 'sincere', 'without wax', 'without pretence'.

But he was probably wrong. Hoad's *Concise Dictionary of English Etymology* says that the English word comes from *sincerus* ('unmixed', 'not hybrid') and so does the *Shorter Oxford English Dictionary* (third edition). And *Webster's Third New International Dictionary* gives a different origin. The Latin is probably from *sem*, 'one', and *creare*, 'create'. To be sincere, in Webster's etymology, is to have an emotion that isn't 'created' or 'manufactured': that isn't, as we might say today, 'insincere'. I have had to dump, regretfully, the 'without wax' idea. It seems as though Barrel was being fanciful. His idea was a 'folk mythology'.

All the same, Barrel's misinformation about 'sincere' delighted me, and alerted me to the fact that words have travelled further than I thought they had. We rarely invent words. Even 'fax' comes from 'facsimile', and 'television' is a Greek/Latin hybrid. 'Bulimia' (Greek 'ox-hunger'), modern as it sounds, is old. 'Computer' is from the Latin *computare* 'to count'. 'Keyboard' is easily traceable and 'screen', streamlined though it sounds, goes back to C15th. Of course there are exceptions. 'Byte', is one example; and surely it is a strange that such a modern word should be followed in the *Collins English Dictionary* by the ubiquitous term 'orig. unkn'.

'Words will ride very slackly at anchor on their etymologies . . . Very few have broken away and drifted from their moorings altogether . . .' Richard Chenevix Trench wrote those words in 1851 (quoted in Crystal & Crystal *Words on Words*). Knowledge of etymology increases our understanding of many subjects, as I think this book makes clear. See for example, my notes on the roots of our language, below. However, as we (subtly or crudely) change objects that we inherit – books, houses, affections, neuroses, attitudes, we also change words too, their spelling, their pronunciation and, gradually, their meanings. So, we must be wary of taking etymology as a guide to what words mean today. Yes, words do 'ride very slackly at anchor on their etymologies'. But they do ride. 'Prevent', for instance, is etymologically 'go before' ('Prevent us, O Lord, in all our doings' – *Book of Common Prayer*) and not 'hinder'. For an example of the dangers of applying what Crystal calls (in *The Cambridge Encyclopedia of the English Language*) 'the etymological fallacy' can be clearly seen in my entries on 'nice' and 'slogan'.

As Samuel Johnson wrote in the introduction to his great dictionary (1755), 'Total and sudden transformations of a language seldom happen, but there are other causes of change which, though slow in their operation, and invisible in their progress, are as much superior to human resistance, as the revolutions of the sky . . .' 'The revolutions of the sky . . .' John McWhorter develops this theme in his book *The Power of Babel*, where he says that language changes like a cloud formation, imperceptibly, for sure, but 'inevitably and completely'.

Nevertheless, the history of words has taken a hold on me, and I am grateful to Barrel. Words are, above all, what help us, above everything, to define ourselves as humans rather than animals. The astonishing ability to communicate in intricate ways; to explain what is wrong with a car engine, and to tell how it is going to be put right; to communicate the most intricate technological processes about computers; to lie while sounding as if we are telling the truth, like a politician or a duplicitous lover; to approach an understanding about what we are in our relationship with ourselves, or with each other, or with our environment, or with nothingness, or with God; to philosophize, to wonder; to be able to utter, at every moment of our waking lives, a new sentence, a sentence never uttered before in the history of the human race (oh yes we can. Here are two: 'Pale goats trample the archdeacon's garden'; and 'The frowning girl and the yellow flower wait for the lover with latte and espresso') boggles any mind. Or it should.

All this is what distinguishes humankind from even the cleverest of the closest mammals. Their communication is limited largely to 'There's danger here' or 'This is my territory, get off it' or 'I want your body to make more creatures like us'. Our words often do mean those things, but mostly, thank goodness, they mean much more, and to be uninterested in those words is to be uninterested in what it is to be human. The death of a language (and they are dying all the time) is just that, a death. And not to care about language, to ignore its importance, is to accept the fact of death without thinking about it.

I have discovered recently that most people are indeed interested in words. All my previous books are about education, especially the teaching of poetry. But these are lead balloon subjects even in most staffrooms, and especially in the pub (though my store of limericks went down well once in The Farrier's Arms in St Albans). I have found, however, that people want to talk about etymology; that (gratifyingly and uniquely) people ask me if they might have a look at drafts of this book as I progress. Language interests us all. I met a 10-year-old the other day who knew, and was pleased to tell everybody, that her name, Zoe, was Greek for life, though I must confess that I've never met a Leah who knew, or was pleased to be told, that her name came from Hebrew 'cow'.

Dr Johnson said that 'a man who does not care about what he puts into himself [meaning what he eats] will not care about anything.' He could also have said that a human being who does not care about what he (or she) speaks, writes and hears will also care about nothing.

To find the roots of our language involves going back to a tribe living north of the Black Sea about 5,000 years ago. That pre-dates Judaism (depending on which event we choose as a starting point) by about 4,000 years, Christianity by about 3,000 and Islam by about 2,500. As that tribe split and drifted, their language split too into many dialects. One thrust of it travelled towards modern India, and the other towards Europe. In Europe, every major language is inherited from that people, except Finnish, Hungarian and Basque. (Such languages are called 'isolates', see p 207).

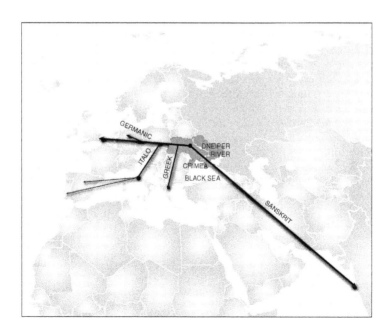

We know almost nothing about the tribe that lived in what is now Ukraine, except through what we know of their language. As Owen Barfield says, in his *History in English Words*, when we trace words back that are common in the family of languages represented in my illustration, we can glimpse a society. Indeed, we can hear it. We can smell it. The early Indo-Europeans kept bees, geese, oxen, sows; they kept hounds; they were fond of a drop (the word 'mead' is everywhere); they used wagons. 'Axle', 'wheel' and 'yoke' are common words in their language, as they are in ours, and in many other languages. But, as Barfield writes, the wheels were solid: there is no common word for 'spoke'.

Only language can bear witness to that. If we want to know these peoples and their history, whose history, after all, is the beginning of ours, archaeology offers nothing. 'Words', as the novelist Ivy Compton-Burnett once wrote, and as the Bee Gees once sang – there's a unique link – 'are all we have'. And you would have to be stony-hearted not to be entranced by the fact that so many words go back so far as to provide a sense of the brotherhood of humankind. The Indo-Europeans looked up at the stars, and used the same word that we do. When I walk round a medieval cathedral, I am always moved by the fact that the flagstones I tread have been worn down by tens of thousands of men and women, whether worshippers, pilgrims or tourists, who have trod there before me.

But the word 'star', *ster* in its Indo-European form, reaches back long before Canterbury Cathedral's flagstones. It reaches back (I have to use my own Judaeo-Christian background here, though this applies to other traditions) through 1950s' popular music about teenage romance ('I see the stars in your eyes . . .'); through Shakespeare writing that love was 'the star to every wandering bark'; through the morning angels singing, under a unique star, on the hill at Bethlehem; through to the time that the Psalms were written; through to the time long, long before the Jewish kingdom was formed; to a time when a member of that obscure tribe pointed up to the heavens at night and said to his or her child something like *sterna*.

We can see how closely these sons and daughters of Indo-European form are related by looking at this table, which shows the names of the first ten numbers in three languages from the family: from left to right, Sanskrit, Latin and Old Irish.

Ekas	unus	oin
Duva	duo	do
Trayas	tres	tri
Catvaras	quattuor	cethair
Panca	quinque	coic
Sat	sex	se

Sapta	septem	secht
Asta	octo	ocht
Nava	novem	noi
Dasa	decem	deich

Source: Encyclopaedia Britannica.

Many of the syllables here are traceable in English, French and other languages. Examples in English are *du*, in our 'double', and *oct*, as in our 'octopus'. You only have to count in French, German or Italian respectively to see this point driven home: 'Un, deux, trios . . . ein, zwei, drei . . . uno, due, tre . . .'

Similarly, here is a basic word in five languages: Hittite (a language spoken by a people that thrived in what is now Turkey 1600–1200 BC), Sanskrit, Greek, Latin, and Old Irish:

kenu, janu, gonu, genu, glun.

The English is 'knee'. We can see all those words, most obviously the Latin, in 'genuflect'. It's also there in 'polygon', 'many-angled': *gonos* is Gk. for 'angle': your calf and your thigh are at an angle to each other every minute of your life, waking or sleeping or, come to that, dead.

But there are many words in our language that are not part of the Indo-European family. Most of these arrived in the returning ships of colonialists, adventurers and pirates, many of them slave-traders. 'Barrack', to mean 'banter', for example, is aboriginal Australian. 'Banana' is from a South American language, brought to us by Portuguese explorers. 'Canoe', which is Haitian, had nothing to do with the Indo-European source. There are hundreds more in this book.

I have to make choices about what to include, and I have chosen, first of all, words about basics: survival, reproduction, death. So food, drink, love, sex and death itself and its rituals, all central to human activity, figure largely. Words about religion, too, are central to the way civilized human beings have thought, and still think, and have spoken and written, and tried to make meaning of their existence. These words are central if only because we quarrel about the subject so much. I have also stressed words about animals: they are also, in their different ways, about survival. For a good reason, naming them was Adam's first act (Gen. 2.19). They serve and feed us, and often are our friends. Then there are the arts: music, painting, poetry, fiction, drama – people in every society relish them; every society has used them to entertain, and to help to move themselves towards an understanding of who we are, both as individuals, and as members of those societies. And there are words about science.

Another criterion for inclusion was simply this: some words are interesting and others aren't. I asked friends what words they would like to see included, and their lists have been a great help. Before that, I made my own list. My book concentrates in concrete words rather than abstract; and if the convolutions of, say, the legal profession are not much in evidence . . . so be it. I admit that I am the kind of man who, looking for the etymology of 'some', finds himself transfixed by 'sorbet', 'soup' and 'spaghetti'.

Bring on the aardvark, I say. (That's another sentence that's never been uttered before.)

A–Z List of Words

A

Aardvark
C19th. f. South African Du. *aard* 'earth' and *vark* 'pig'.

Ab-
This L. prefix denotes 'away', 'from' or 'off'. So 'abhor', C15th., *horrere* 'shudder', so 'shudder away'.

Aborigine
C16th. Nothing, etymologically, to do with Australia. *Aborigines* were believed to be the first inhabitants of Italy: f. L. *ab* + *origine* 'beginning'.

Absinthe
C17th. f. Gk. *apsinthion* through L. 'wormwood', 'bitter herb'. f. a non-IE. root, and therefore obscure.

Academy
C16th. Gk. *akademeia* was a gymnasium (school) near Athens, named after the hero Academus. Plato (whence its fame) taught there in C4th. BC. The word comes to us through L. *academia*.

Ace
C13th. f. L. *ac*, a coin.

Acid
C17th. f. L. *acidus* 'sharp', which is also the source of the last part of >vinegar. *Acus* = needle. There is an IE. root 'be pointed'.

Acrobat
C19th. f. Gk. *akrobatos* 'walking on tiptoe'. The IE. root in the previous entry is visible here: an acrobat's toes are pointed.

Act
C14th. f. L. *actus* 'doing'. So 'action' and 'actor'. The meaning for 'stage player' emerged C16th.

Add
C14th. f. L. *addere*.

Adder
OE. *nadder*, which meant any snake. It lost its initial consonant, and eventually became an (the indefinite article 'a' taking on the 'n') adder, meaning >viper. This happened to other words. >umpire and >apron.

Adieu
C14th. f. Fr. *a Dieu*. Old Christian blessings linger inside words like these. >Goodbye.

Admiral
C13th. to mean 'Arab ruler'; f. Arab. 'commander'.

Adultery
C16th. This is nothing to do with 'adult', even though only adults commit it. f. L. *adulterare*, 'corruption'.

Age
C13th. f. L. *aevum* 'age of time'.

Aggravate
C16th. The root here is L. *gravus* 'heavy', and the original meaning was 'to add weight', but since C16th., it means 'incense', even 'annoy' as in 'This stupid computer is aggravating me.' See McWhorter (2001) for a convincing account of how language is never static in either its meanings or in other ways, such as pronunciation. Thus a purist account of linguistic 'correctness' flies in the face of reality.

Agnostic
Invented by T H Huxley, Br. biologist (1825–1895) in 1869 f. the negative Gk. *a* and *gnosis* 'knowledge'.

Agoraphobia
>-phobia

Agriculture
C15th. f. L. *agricultura*.

Akimbo
C18th. This odd word, meaning 'with hands on hips and elbows sticking out' (note that you cannot have legs akimbo) comes f. ON. *i keng boginn* 'bent in a curve'.

Albino
C18th. Many words come f. L. *albus*, 'white'. This comes through *albo*, the Port. equivalent. Other *alb-* words include: 'Albion', OE., an old name for Britain, and refers to the white cliffs of Dover; 'album', C17th.; 'albumen', C17th., 'egg white'.

Alcohol
C16th. Like many 'al-' words, this one comes to us f. Arab., in this case *al-kul*. The root of the second part is *khol* 'powder used for darkening the eyes'. Gradually the meaning changed to the familiar one today: 'essence . . . distillation of'. Other examples are: 'alkali', C14th., and 'alembic', C14th., 'apparatus for distilling'. The Arabs were advanced in chemistry, as they were in mathematics (>algebra). *Al* is the definite article. >Allah.

Ale
OE. f. ON. *ealu*, the northern European word for the cup that both cheers and inebriates. It comes ultimately, through Scand., f. an IE. word for 'bitter'. >Beer for the usual Germanic and southern European word, but note that the Portuguese and Spanish have a different word altogether, *cerveza*, f. the word for 'wheat', which English has in 'cereal'.

Al fresco
C18th. It. for 'in the fresh [air]' or (about painting) 'on the fresh [plaster]'. When we have a picnic, we lunch or dine 'al fresco'. But, as Bryson 1990 points out, Italians now use it to mean 'in prison'. My friend Tony thinks that this is a joke. 'Where is Tony, your wild friend?' [wry look] 'He is *al fresco*.' Much as in English, we might once have said, 'He is a guest of Her Majesty.'

Algebra
C16th. As well as chemists (>alcohol), the Arabs were pioneering mathematicians. This first meant 'the mending of bones' (used like that in 1541). Presumably, the mathematical activity was seen as a restoration of order, like the mending of bones.

Allah
C18th. 'The God'. Arabic, obviously.

Alleluia
>Hallelujah

Alligator
C17th. f. Sp. *el largarto* 'the lizard'.

Alphabet
C16th. f. the first two words of the Gk. alphabet, *alpha* and *beta*. There was, in the same century, an attempt to restrict the word to mean the Greek alphabet, and to use *ABC* for the English. It didn't take on.

Amateur
C18th. f. L. *amor* 'love'. Thus to be an amateur at a sport was to do it for love. Now, it is to be inept; in cricket parlance, a 'rabbit'; as in 'That was amateurish shot'. >amorous.

Amazon
C14th. This word, for one of a race of female warriors, has an old folk mythology. It was believed that it came f. the Gk. *a mazos* without a breast, and that these fearsome women mutilated themselves to facilitate drawing a bow. In fact, it comes from the name of a Scythian tribe. The Sp. soldier Francisco de Orellana gave the river its name when reporting battles with female warriors.

Ambulance
C19th. f. L. *ambulare* 'walk'. Originally, an 'ambulance' was a field ambulance. It is not a hospital for the walking wounded: it is a walking hospital.

Amen
OE. Heb. 'truth', 'agreement'.

American
C16th. f. the name of It. navigator *Amerigo* Vespucci (1454–1512) who travelled there three times and claimed to have discovered it.

Amethyst
C13th. f. Gk. *a* 'not' and *methustos*, f. *methu* wine. It was thought in ancient times that anyone wearing or touching an amethyst could avoid drunkenness, and wine goblets were sometimes decorated with it.

Amoeba
C19th. f. Gk. *amoibe* 'changing'.

Amok, amuck
C17th. f. Malay *amoq* furious assault. The spelling *amuck* reflects the word's pronunciation.

Amorous
C14th. f. L. *amor* 'love'. >amateur.

Ampere
C19th. The unit of electric current is named after the Fr. physicist Andre *Ampere* (1775–1836).

Anchor
OE. f. Gk. *agkura*, through L.

Anchovy
C16th. f. Sp., Port., *anchova*, *anchoa*. Beyond that, the origin is disputed. The first use is in Falstaff's accounts, stolen from his wallet, in *Henry IV Part 1* 2:4: 'Item anchovies and sack [liquor] after supper'.

Angel
C12th. f. Gk. *aggelos*, 'messenger'; a translation of Heb. *mal'akh*.

Anger
C12th. f. ON. *angr*, 'grief'; by C14th, it had its present meaning.

Angle
C14th. f. Gk. *agkulos* 'bent'. The name of the tribe, C18th. (and ultimately the name England) is the same word and comes from the place name *Angul* in present day Schleswig, so named because of its shape. So Anglican, C17th.

Animal
C14th. f. L. *anima* 'breath' and therefore 'life'. The word 'animus', meaning 'hostile spirit', is C19th.

Ankle
C14th. Has an IE. root; comes to us through Germanic languages.

Anonymous
C17th. f. Gk. but going back further into IE. Gk. *an* 'without' + *onoma*. >name.

Anorak
C20th. Rarely among English words, f. Greenland Inuit *anoraq*, a piece of clothing. The meaning 'nerd' or, more kindly, 'studious person' is late C20th.

Anorexia
C16th. *anorexy* meaning 'want of appetite'. f. Gk. *an-* 'without' and *orexis*, 'appetite'.

Ant
OE. A Germanic word; ModGer. is *Ameise*.

Ante-
This L. prefix denotes 'before'. So 'antenatal', C20th. is 'before birth'. It shouldn't be confused with . . .

Anti-
which is a Gk. prefix denoting 'against'. So 'anti-aircraft', C20th., etc.

Anus
C15th. f. L. 'ring'.

Ape
OE. A Germanic word. Ger. is *Affe*.

Aphrodisiac
C18th. f. the name of the Gk. goddess of love, Aphrodite.

Apple
OE. A 'brother/sisterhood-word': one of those, like >arse, >axe, >brother, >father >mother, >sister, >star and hundreds of others, many in this book,

that exist in one form or another all over the family of IE. languages. It comes to us f. the OE *aeppel*, and was originally applied to fruits in general.

Apricot

C16th. This word has travelled. *Praecox* was L. for 'early ripening'; through Gk., it came to Arab.: *al-birquq*. Thence it came back to Europe as Port. *albricoque*. Albuquerque got its names from the Sp. who had the word from the Port. It is, therefore, 'The Apricot City'.

Apron

C14th. f. OFr. *nappe* 'table-cloth'. The word was *napron*. >adder, >umpire for other words that have lost their 'n' to the indefinite article.

Aquamarine

C18th. This comes f. *aqua*, 'water', and *marina*, sea, both L. So: 'green like >sea >water'. Other words f. L. *aqua*: 'aquarium', C19th.; 'aquatic' C15th; an 'aqueduct', C16th., carries water.

Arctic

C14th. f. Gk. *arktikos* 'bear', f. the name of the constellation.

Arena

C17th. f. L. *harena* 'sand'; possibly of Etruscan or Sabine origin.

Aristocracy

C16th. f. Gk. *aristos* 'best' and *cracy* 'rule'. >democracy.

Armadillo

C16th. f. Sp. *armado* is 'armed man', so this word means 'little armed man'. Compare our use of *-ette* as a suffix to denote a small version of something larger, as in *maisonette*, C19th., 'little house'.

Armageddon

f. the Authorised Version of the Bible. This word for the last decisive battle between good and evil comes f. Heb. *har meggidon* 'the mountain district of Meggigo' where battles took place in Old Testament times.

Arse

OE. Obsolete, says *Shorter Oxford English Dictionary* (*SOED*). I don't think so. A brother/sisterhood word. >axe, >brother, >father >mother, >sister, >star. It exists in perhaps every IE. language, f. the Old Irish *err*, 'tail', to the Armenian *or*, 'rump'. 'Wheatear', the bird, comes from 'white arse' because of its white tail feathers. I am looking at a picture of a wheatear as I write, and that derivation sounds inappropriate, if not downright disrespectful.

Arsenal
C16th. Goes back to Arab *dar-sina a*, 'factory'. Emerging in It. as *arsenale*, it meant 'dockyard'.

Art
C15th. f. L. *ars*, 'craftsmanship'. There is an IE. root, *ar-*, which means putting things together. The idea that art is a matter of waiting for inspiration is relatively recent, post-Romantic in fact. >Poem.

Artichoke
C16th. The name of this thistle-related plant with edible parts comes ultimately f. Arab. *al-karsufa* through Sp. and It. >Jerusalem artichoke.

Arty-farty
C20th. An obvious reduplication of 'art' usually used to mock supposedly artistic types. >namby-pamby.

Asparagus
C16th. f. Gk. *asparagus*. There was a folk etymology that leads to the spurious 'sparrow grass' that has died out.

Assassin
C16th. f. Arab. *hassasin*, a smoker of hashish. At the time of the Crusades, there were, we are told, men pledged to kill. They did it under the influence of hashish. Though not necessarily: Hitchings writes that the word comes f. the Hashshashin group who preyed on caliphs of a different persuasion. Travellers came back with the earlier myth.

Astrology
C14th. >star, >-logy.

Astronomy
C13th. ME. >star, >-nomy.

Atheism
>theism

Atlantic
see next . . .

Atlas
C16th. The Flemish cartographer Mercator (1512–1594) used this word, the name of a Roman god who held the world up, and it has stuck as the meaning of a book of maps. Thus also 'Atlantic', C15th.

Atonement
C16th. The state of being 'at one'. A rare thing, a theological word that comes f. A-S. Such words rarely survive, L. or Gk. words being preferred; in this case, 'reconciliation' (L.). There were other attempts to use

A-S. words: one translation of the New Testament includes 'mooned' for >lunatic, 'hundreder' for 'centurion' and 'freshman' f. 'proselyte', a new believer. They didn't catch on, but 'atonement' did. So did >worship. 'Atone' is a back formation.

Attic
C18th. f. the Gk. place name *Attica*, whose style of architecture influenced the structure.

Aubergine
C18th. f. Pers. *badingan*, through Arab. *al-bainjan*, then Catalonian *alberginia*. The word *brinjal*, familiar to many of us from visits to curry houses, has the same Sanskr. root. It only looks different because it lacks the Arab. definite article *al-* at the beginning. Hitchings writes that the term *brown jolly* is used in the Caribbean. The Arab.-derived word has more dignity than that one, or *eggplant* (US English).

Autocracy
C17th. >democracy

Autograph
>graph words

Avalanche
C18th. f. Fr. *avaler* 'descend' and Swiss dialect word *lavanche*, of obscure origin.

Aviary
C16th. f. L. *avis* 'bird'.

Avocado
C17th. f. the Nahuatl Indians' language *ahuacatl*, 'testicle', presumably from the resemblance in shape, if not in size. The Spaniards used a folk etymology, converting the word into an easier form, 'avocado', which meant 'advocate'. >orchid. *SOED* omits the testicle part of this. For other words f. this source >chilli, >chocolate.

Axe
OE. is *aex*. A brother/sisterhood word. >arse, >brother, >father, >mother, >sister, >star. Note Ger. *Axt*, Du. *aaks*, L. *ascia*, Gk. *axine*. Humankind has always needed such a tool, and such a word.

Ayatollah
C20th. A leader in the >Shiite sect of >Islam. Arab., through Pers., f. *aya* 'sign' and *allah* 'the God'.

B

Baba

C14th. like 'baby', prob. imit. of an infant's babbling.

Babble

C15th. may be imitative of baby-talk, and/or f. the L. *babulus*, 'fool'.

Bacchanal

C16th. 'Drunken riot' named after Gk. name *Bakchos*, then L. *Bacchus*, the god of wine.

Bachelor

C13th. a word of many related meanings, from 'young knight' to 'graduate' and to its present meaning, C14th. It is of obscure origin, though Webster suggests it may be related to Gael. *bachlach* 'peasant'.

Bacon

C14th. a Germanic word, with a root in a word for 'back'. There was an OE. word, 'flitch'. Dunmow, in Essex, is a 'flitch town'. If a married couple could show that their marriage was happy after a year, they were awarded a side of pig – a flitch. Otherwise flitch is now obsolete, though no doubt there are marriages contracted in Dunmow that are still happy after a year.

Bad

C13th. Like >badge, >blizzard, >dog and many others, this is a word we know practically nothing about, and has cognates in no other language. It may come from a derogatory word for 'man behaving in a >homosexual manner'; possibly with roots in an OE. word *baddael*, 'hermaphrodite'.

Badge

C14th. of unknown origin.

Badger

From C16th. onwards, this word of unknown origin (>badge is a blind alley here, though it may refer to the white mark on the animal's forehead) has displaced the Celt. word 'brock', though that word has survived as a generic nickname. f. Celt. *broc*, 'stinking fellow'.

Badminton
C19th. f. the name of the Duke of Beaufort's house.

Bagel
C20th. f. Yid. *beygl*, related to OHG. *biogan* 'bend'. The shape is the deciding factor here, as with >croissant.

Baksheesh
C17th. f. Pers. word for 'give', through Turkish, Arab. and Hindi.

Ballyhoo
C20th. US. Origin unknown, though *SOED* suggests that it is the name of a Central American wood of poor quality: the boats made from it failed.

Baloney
C20th. US. It is assumed, without much evidence, that it comes f. the name of the It. city Bologna and its sausage.

Balti
C20th. Urdu 'bucket'.

Bamboozle
C18th. Origin unknown. Jonathan Swift mentions it in a list of words 'Banter, Bamboozle . . . struggling for the vogue' in the magazine *The Tatler*. There are always, despite what purists would prefer, new words coming into the language.

Banal
C19th. f. OFr. *banal* which referred to the bakery etc. that the lord owned, and which all his tenants had to use.

Banana
C16th. *Via* Sp. and Port. travellers, f. Central Africa.

Bankrupt
C16th. *Banca* was the It. money-lender's bench (whence we get 'bank', C15th.); and *rotta* is It. 'broken' (whence we get 'rupture'). When the unfortunate man went bust, his bench was broken.

Baptist
ME. f. Gk. 'dip'. Thus John the Baptist in the New Testament, who immersed his followers in water. The Baptist denomination still practises full immersion.

Barbarian
C16th. f. Gk. *barbaros*, 'foreign, rude'. Cf. the name Barbara, 'wild girl'. Some writers suggest that sophisticated Greeks heard outsiders' speech as 'ba-ba-ba'. A folk mythology says that the word comes f. L. *barba* 'beard'.

Barbecue

C17th. f. Haitian *barbacoa*, 'crate on posts', through Sp.

Barber

C13th. f. L. *barba* 'beard'. >Barbarian.

Bard

C14th. f. Ir. Gael. This Celt. word goes back 2000 years, meaning something like 'poet-singer'.

Baroque

C19th. This word for an ornate style in art and architecture has two possible and mutually exclusive derivations: (1) It is named after an It. painter Federigo Barocci (1528–1612); (2) f. Port. *barroco* 'irregularly shaped pearl'.

Barrack

There are two Eng. words: the first, C17th., is f. Sp. *barraca* 'soldier's tent'. The second C19th. is f. Aboriginal Australian *borak* 'banter'.

Bastard

C13th. Origin unknown; but some suggest that it derives f. Fr. *fils de bast*, literally 'back-saddle son', a son begotten in a casual manner. Webster derives it, equally picturesquely, f. 'son of the barn'. The word's use as a term of abuse, much weakened in recent years as illegitimacy has become respectable, dates from C19th. Note that in Shakespeare's *King John*, the word serves simply as title for Philip. The picture is more nuanced for Edmond in *King Lear*, but is still neutral. Johnson says the word is of Welsh origin, and gives *bastardd*, but this is almost certainly wrong.

Bath

OE. a Germanic word. OHG. is *bad*, reflected in names of spa towns in Germany, such as *Bad Endorf*; like our 'Bath'.

Bawd

C14th. abbr. of *bawdstrot* 'procurer', f. OFr. The first part comes f. a word meaning 'lively', the second f. one meaning 'old woman'.

Bazaar

C16th. Ult. f. the Pers. *bazar*, 'market'.

Beach

C16th. Of unknown origin, though *Chambers* identifies an OIce. word *bekkr*.

Bed

OE. A Germanic word present in ModGer. *Bett*, of unc. orig. Rom. languages have different words: *lit* in Fr., *letto* in It., *cama*, Sp.

Bedad

C18th. Ir. A polite evasion of 'by God'. The language is freckled with these terms. *Jeez*, US, is an obvious one. *Zounds* is Tudor for 'God's wounds'. I once heard, many years ago, a French schoolgirl exclaim in surprise *mercredi!* [Wednesday] and asked: 'You mean *merde*? [>shit]'. She had. So other languages have them too. Other polite evasions: 'For crying out loud'; and the now more-or-less obsolete 'Good Grief' and 'My Goodness'. 'Sweet Fanny Adams' is a polite evasion ('SFA', 'sweet fuck all').

Bedlam

C15th. The Hospital of St Mary of Bethlehem in London was founded in 1247 for the care of what we would now call the 'mentally ill'. It was built 'originally' (Hoad tells us, distressingly) 'for the entertainment of the bishop and canons'. The word is a contraction of 'Bethlehem'. Hence it became a word for any lunatic asylum, and now it has dropped to the meaning of a 'noisy, confused situation'. 'My classroom', a teacher will say, 'was absolute bedlam today'.

Beef

C13th. Note that we retain the old Saxon word for *ox*, but we have here the Norman word *boef* for the meat it gives. This is because the Saxon tending the cattle in the field saw little or nothing of the meat which his Norman masters scoffed in the kitchen. This is a fine example of words exposing a social reality. The poor Saxon had the word connected to his work, the rich Norman had the word connected to his pleasure. The same happened with >pork and >veal. But Bryson quotes Burchfield here: this distinction between 'field names and food names' is 'an enduring myth'. And Hitchings lays the blame for it at the door of Sir Walter Scott's *Ivanhoe*. 'Bully beef' is an English soldier's try at the Fr. *boef bouilli*.

Beer

OE. The southern European and Germanic word (*biere*, Fr., *birra*, It., *bier*, German) for the cup that both cheers and inebriates. f. L. *bibere*, 'drink'. But the Scand. word is >ale. We, uniquely, have both.

Begum

C19th. A surname for Islamic women. f. Urdu *begam* 'woman of high rank'.

Belfry

C13th. There is no etymological connection between this and >bell. This word comes from Germanic roots, one, the first part, meaning 'protect' and the other 'peace': a belfry was a protective shelter. The word began to be used for 'bell tower', C15th., because of the similarity between the words.

Belief, believe

OE. I was told by preachers when I was a young man that these words stemmed from 'living by', but it doesn't. The root is in OHG., and denotes 'hold trust in'.

Bell

OE. Most European languages have words related to our 'clock' (*cloche* in Fr., for example, *Glocke* in Ger.). There is no known certain source for our word, though it may be related to OHG. *bellan* 'roar'. >belfry.

Belly

OE. f. a Germanic word for 'bag'.

Berk

C20th. An example of rhyming slang that has stuck. 'Berkshire Hunt', with the first word pronounced as spelt, not 'bark'. I have never heard anyone say, except facetiously, 'I'm going to make a cup of rosy [Rosy Lee: tea] and go up the old apples [apples and pears: stairs] with me old pot [pot and pan: man].' I have probably been called, behind my back, a 'berk'. But 'Mutt and Geoff' (two forgotten cartoon characters) means 'deaf' and is widespread. So are 'Sherman tank' and 'Barclay's Bank'. So is 'bottle', meaning courage: 'bottle and glass'. Footballers, when they have a bad game, call it a 'Lionel': f. 'Lionel Blair', a dancer, + 'mare' (shortening of 'nightmare').

Berry

OE. f. OHG. *beri*. The word is only present in Germanic languages.

Bi-

This L. prefix is one of many stems f. IE. for duality: *dui*, Gk., *dvi*, Sanskr. So 'bigamous', (Gk. *gamos* 'married') C13th., though we should not assume there will be merely two spouses; 'bisexual', C20th., (only two sexes, though); 'biplane', C20th.; and 'biscuit', C14th., 'twice-baked'. >bicycle.

Bible

C13th. Ultimately f. Gk. *biblia* 'books'. And thus, 'bibliophile', C19th., 'lover of books', Gk. >phil. 'friend'. *Biblia a biblia*, f. this word and a Gk. negative, is a Victorian phrase for 'books that are not books', for example, books about royalty on horseback, biographies of footballers still in their early twenties, celebrity cookbooks etc.

Bicycle

C19th. f. L. root >bi and Gk. *kuklos* 'wheel'. There were objections to this use of classical languages: the poet William Barnes (1801–1886) suggested that the invention should be called 'wheel-saddle'. >atonement, >worship for A-S. words that did survive.

Big
C13th. of unknown origin, but possibly Scand.

Bigamy
>bi-

Bigot
C16th. f. an old Fr. word for 'hypocrite'. Beyond that, origin unknown.

Bikini
C20th. According to Ayto, the explosion of the atom bomb in the Bikini atoll in the Pacific was hardly less explosive on American airmen than the sight of the first two-piece bathing costumes on female bathers.

Bio-
This Gk. prefix denotes 'life'. 'Biography', C17th., is 'written account of a life'. >graph. So 'biology', C19th., is 'study of living things'. >logy.

Bird
OE. *brid*. A mystery word that has no relatives in any IE. language. The word used was originally 'fowl', which is still there in the old rhyme: 'All the fowls of the air / Fell and sighin' and sobbin' . . .'

Birth
C12th. f. OIce. *burthre*.

Bizarre
C17th. f. Fr. 'odd'; before that Sp. *bazarro* 'brave'. There was a Basque word *bizar* 'beard'. It. *bizzarro* was once 'angry', but now the word has the same meaning as in Eng.

Black
C13th. The original word was *swart*, which we still have in 'swarthy' and Ger. has in *schwartz*. f. ON. *blakrr*, confused in ME. later with *blak* 'pale', f. which we get 'bleak'.

Blarney
C18th. 'Cajoling talk'. f. the name of a village near Cork in Ireland. Kissing a stone in a castle there helps one to become skilful in flattery. In his novel *The Vicar of Wakefield* (1766), Oliver Goldsmith gives the name Lady Blarny to a smooth-talker.

Blaspheme
C14th. means, today, something like 'to take the name of the Lord in vain': to swear with his name. But it comes f. Gk. word meaning 'speak [*phemos*] evil or profane things [*blas*]', f. a word meaning 'hurtful': a far more general definition.

Bless
OE. Fr. *blesser* means 'wound'. 'Bless' in the Eng. sense is unique, and meant originally to 'mark with blood' (so the blood connection is there) thereby conferring sanctity. The word's sense of happiness ('God bless you!') is over a thousand years old, and is prob. f. a confusion with >bliss.

Blighty
C20th. In his World War I poem 'The Chances', Wilfred Owen has a soldier say that 'next time please I'll thank [God] for a blighty', meaning a wound that isn't life-threatening, but that will get him sent home to England. The word comes f. the Hindi *bilayati*, 'home', and was picked up by the British during the Raj; orig. f. Arabic, *wilayat* 'district'.

Bliss
OE. f. a Germanic word. >bless.

Blizzard
C19th. The first user, according to Bryson, seems to have been the 'wild frontier man' Davy Crockett (1829). It meant 'sharp blow or shock'. By 1870, it had taken on its current snowy, freezing, dangerous meaning; of unknown origin.

Blood
OE. a Germanic word: for example, Ger. *Blut*. The southern European languages take their words f. the L. *sanguis*, whence our 'sanguine'. Gk. had *haima*, hence our 'haemorrhage' and 'haemophiliac'.

Bloody
As expletive, C17th. The notion that it came f. a blasphemous 'By our Lady' usage is prob. a folk etymology. Blood itself was enough to supply an intensifying adjective.

Bloomers
C19th. after Amelia Bloomer (1818–1894), a pioneering feminist who wore these long loose trousers.

Blue
C13th. Although there is an IE. word, it meant 'yellow'. We get our word in its present meaning, indirectly, f. Fr. *bleu*. Colour words often change their meaning. >green.

Bobby
C19th. The London policeman gets his name from Sir Robert Peel (1788–1850), Home Secretary when the Metropolitian Police Force was formed. Other terms for policemen are obscure, though the out-of-date 'peeler' also refers to Sir Robert. Ayto and Simpson offer 'rozzer', 1893–, 'fuzz', 1929–, 'filth' 1967– 'Bill' 1970–, all of unknown origin.

Body

OE. *bodig*. Of obscure origin, and with no IE. cousins, although OHG. has *botah*. Fr., Sp., It. use words f. L. *corpus*, from which we get our 'corpse', C14th. and *corpus*, for 'body of writings'.

Bogus

C19th., US., applied orig. to a machine for producing false money, and then to the money itself. Origin unknown, say most books, but Hitchings suggests that it's f. Hausa, a West African language.

Bomb

C17th. Almost certainly imit., and traceable back to Gk. *bombos* 'humming, booming'.

Bonbon

C19th. f. Fr. 'good-good', ult. f. L. *bonus* 'good'.

Bonfire

C14th. orig. a 'bone-fire'.

Booby

C17th. A modern-sounding word, but f. L. *balbus*, through Sp. *bobo*, both 'stammering'. Imit.

Boomerang

C19th. f. Dharuk, the language of the aborigines of New South Wales.

Boot

C14th. f. ON. *boti*. Origin obscure, though Fr. has *botte*.

Booze

C13th. f. MD. *buizen*, 'drink too much'. It has been going on a long time. See Gen. 9.20–21, where Noah plants a vineyard, drinks the wine, gets drunk and inadvertently exposes himself, all in the space of two verses.

Bore

'What a bore!': this sense comes from the C18th, when at some point it became a fashionable usage; of obscure origin. Such faddish words at various times include 'swell', C18th; 'fab', C20th; and 'wicked' (current, at least among children, to mean 'good'.)

Boss

C19th. to mean master. Origin US., f. Du. *baas*, of unknown origin, as is the (unconnected) C13th. word meaning 'protuberance'.

Bother

C18th. of unknown origin though perhaps f. Irish *bodhrain*, 'commotion', or *bodhair* 'deafen'. *Chambers* points out that the earliest uses of the word in Eng. Literature are in works by Irishmen: Sheridan, Swift and Sterne.

Bottle
C14th. f. late L. *buttis*, 'cask', whence our 'butt', 'barrel'. The meaning 'courage' is rhyming slang, 'bottle and glass'. For more rhyming slang >berk.

Bottom
OE. It's everywhere in the IE. languages, and Eng. gets it f. the Germanic branch. The base IE. word also leads to L. *fundus*, from which Eng. gets 'foundation', 'fundament' etc. By C18th., it takes on the meaning 'buttocks'.

Bourbon
C19th. The whiskey (>whisky) is named after Bourbon County, Kentucky, US, where it was first made.

Bowlderize
C19th. Troubled by the filth, as he saw it, in Shakespeare, Thomas Bowdler published in 1818 a version 'in which . . . those words and expressions are omitted which cannot with propriety be read aloud in a family . . .' For example, Iago doesn't tell Othello that Cassio and Desdemona are 'making the beast with two backs', but that they are 'now together'. Thus all literary prudery is open to the charge that bears his name.

Box
C14th. meaning 'hit', of unknown origin. The earlier word, OE., 'receptacle' is f. L. *buxidem*, a variation of *pyxis*, which we have in 'pyx', a container for the Host at the Communion service.

Boy
C13th. f. Gk. *bous* 'ox'. The explanation is that the word orig. meant 'man-servant'; so 'in fetters', like an ox. From C14th., the word has its present meaning.

Boycott
In 1880, the Irish Land League ostracized certain agents of British colonialism, and Captain Boycott was one of them.

Brahmin
C14th. A member of the priestly or learned class of Hindus. Sansk. *Brahman* 'priest'.

Braille
Named after its inventor, Louis Braille (1809–1852).

Brandy
C17th. f. Du. *brandewijn*, 'burned wine'.

Brave
C15th. f. L. *barbarus*. Somewhere between Sp. *bravo* 'wild' and Fr. *brave* 'valiant' the word moved from the negative to the positive.

Brawl
C14th. origin unknown, though it does convey that sense of pulling and shoving on the pavement outside a pub when too much football has been celebrated or mourned, and too much bitter ale, lager and shorts have been necked. In other words, it is imit.

Bread
OE. a Germanic word of unknown origin. Ger. has *Brot*. It replaced the earlier word, 'loaf'. Dizzy Gillespie (jazz trumpeter) first used it for 'money' (1930s).

Break
OE. A Germanic (Ger. *Brechen*) word that goes back to an IE. root whence L. *frangere*.

Breakfast
C15th. When you eat the first meal of the day, you 'break your fast'.

Breast
OE *breost*. There is an IE. base. Descendants include Irish *bru*, 'womb'. The central notion is of swelling, of both breast and belly, during pregnancy.

Breath
OE. to mean 'odour'. Ult. f. an IE. base meaning 'burn, heat', it found its modern sense in C14th.

Breeze
C16th. meaning 'north-east wind', which is what Sp. *brisa* means. Current meaning also C16th.

Brew
OE. f. an IE. root meaning 'heat'.

Bric-a-brac
C19th. f. Fr. *a bric et la brac* 'all over the place'; of unknown origin.

Bride
OE. isn't traceable to IE., but in all Germanic languages it means the same. 'Bridal' comes f. 'bride-ale'. The second part of 'Bridegroom', OE. *brydguma*, is f. a word for 'man', related to L. *homo*, and nothing to do with looking after horses.

Bridge
OE. *brycg*. A Germanic word: Ger. *Brucke*. Rom. Languages have words f. L. *Pontus*, and Welsh is *pont*. The name for the card game is of unknown origin.

Brinjal
>aubergine

Britain
f. L. *Brittones*, the Romans' name for the tribe who lived in these islands.

Broccoli
C17th. Plural of It. *broccolo* 'cabbage sprout'. Also, the name of the producer of several James Bond movies (Harry).

Brock
>Badger

Brogue
C16th. meaning 'a strong outdoor shoe', f. Gael. *brog*. C17th. to mean 'strong accent': it may be a facetious allusion to the footwear.

Brontosaurus
C19th. f. Gk. *bronte* 'thunder' and *sauros* 'lizard'.

Brothel
C14th. 'worthless fellow'. C15th., 'prostitute'. C16th., 'bawdy-house', 'house of ill repute' etc. f. OE. *brothen*, 'gone to ruin'.

Brother
OE. a basic word. The Brotherhood of Man, indeed. It's *bhrater, frater, frere, phrater, bhratr, brothar, bruder, broeder, broder,* respectively in Northern India, Italy (Latin), France, Greece, Sanskrit (India), Germany (*brother* and *bruder*), The Netherlands and Sweden. It is *brawd* in Mod. Welsh. The word is a survivor from our earliest linguistic ancestor, IE. The It./L. form *frater*, f. the same root, survives in our 'fraternal'.

Brown
OE. Widespread among the NGer. and Scand. languages, it is related to 'burnish', which reflects its original meaning.

Brutal
C15th. f. L. for 'heavy', and referred to stupidity of animals. Why the name became attached to a noble Roman family is unclear. Hamlet puns excruciatingly on this name (3:2 of Shakespeare's play).

Buckshee
>baksheesh

Budgerigar
C19th. f. Australian Aborigine. for 'good' and 'cockatoo', not as Charles Causley writes in his poem 'One day at a Perranporth Petshop' 'good food'.

Bugger

C16th. f. the MedL. for 'Bulgarians' who, being Eastern Orthodox rather than Roman Catholic, were considered heretics, the original meaning of this word. The Albigensian heretics inherited the name, and they were believed to be largely homosexual; has slowly morphed into its present insulting meaning. Though note, it has morphed again into a term of affection. 'Hello, you old bugger, how're you doing?'

Bulimia

C20th. f. Gk. *bous* 'ox' (>boy) and *limon* 'hunger'.

Bulletin

C17th. A 'bull' is a pronouncement f. the Pope, named after L. *bulla* 'seal'. So, a 'little bull', the meaning has now much widened.

Bully

C16th. In Shakespeare's *A Midsummer Night's Dream* 3:1, Quince calls Bottom 'bully bottom', meaning a 'fine fellow', rather like our 'good bloke'. The word also meant >sweetheart; by C17th., it had its present meaning.

Bum

C14th. meaning the buttocks, is of obscure origin. But for the meaning 'tramp', C19th. it comes f. Ger. *Bummein stroll*. Hence the title of Jerome K Jerome's (1859–1927) less successful follow-up to *Three Men in a Boat*, *Three Men on the Bummel*.

Bumf

C19th. f. the earlier 'bumfodder'; this orig. meant 'toilet paper', but now means 'useless bits of paper' with which anyone in education, the police or the health service will be familiar. Had the 'paperless office', predicted by technocrats in the 1970s, actually come about, the word would now be obsolete.

Bungalow

C17th. f. Hindi *bangla* 'pertaining to Bengal'.

Bunk

Both meanings 'sleeping berth' and 'make off', each C19th., have unknown origins.

Bunkum

C19th. US. Felix Walker was an obscure Congressman who represented Buncombe County, North Carolina (1817–1823). His excuse for a pointless and rambling speech was that he had to speak 'for the people of Buncombe'.

Burqa

C20th. f. Arab.

Bus
C19th. short for 'omnibus', *omni* being L. for 'all'; first used for horse-drawn vehicles.

Butterfly
OE. Many believe that this derives f. 'flutter by'. This >Spoonerism (or metathesis, to use the technical term for the swapping of sounds) is a folk etymology. It is f. words for 'butter' and 'fly'. It was believed that the insect fed on butter.

BYOG
C20th. Aust. and NZ. for 'unlicensed restaurant'. Acrostic for '**B**ring **Y**our **O**wn **G**rog'.

C

Cab
C19th. short for Fr. *cabriolet* and earlier It. *capriolare* 'leap'; the original single horse-drawn vehicle was springy.

Cabbage
C14th. f. OF. *caboche* 'head'.

Cabbala
C16th. an oral Jewish tradition handed down f. Moses; f. Heb. *kibbel* 'receive'.

Caboodle
C19th. US. a contraction of 'whole kit and boodle'; the latter word f. Du. *boedel* 'all one's possessions'.

Cack-handed
C19th. When my father called me this to mean that I was clumsy, he didn't know that the origin of the first part was an IE. root, from which many languages get words to do with excrement. >poppycock. Clumsy people make a mess. And note the tradition in many cultures, the left hand is used to clean oneself. Also, >left is often connected with ominous feelings, as in the north side of a churchyard (left as you face the altar and the rising sun).

Cactus
C17th. f. Gk. *kaktos*, an edible prickly plant. The name in the modern sense was used in 1767 by Linneaus in his plant classification.

Caddie
As golfer's attendant C18th. f. Fr. *cadet*, 'young soldier'.

Caesarean
C17th. In Shakespeare's *Macbeth*, Macduff tells Macbeth (who can't be killed by 'man of woman born') before he slaughters him, that he was 'from his mother's womb / Untimely ripp'd': presumably signifying a Caesarean birth, as Julius Caesar was, according to legend. One of

Shakespeare's weaker plot devices, alongside Burnham Wood arriving at Dunsiname in the same play.

Café
C19th. f. It. *caffe* 'coffee'.

Caliph
C14th. This word for a successor of the prophet is f. Arab. *kalofa* 'succeed'.

Callipygian
C19th. The first part is f. Gk. *kallos* 'beautiful', the second fr. *pyge* 'buttocks'. In today's terms it means 'having a nice bum'.

Calm
C14th. ult. f. Gk. *kauma* 'heat of the day'. This developed into meaning something like a siesta, and then its present meaning emerged.

Camel
OE. Semitic, f. Heb. *gamal*, and Arab. *jamal*. Thence in Gk. *kamelos* and L. *camelus*.

Camera
C18th. L. 'a vaulted room'. In photography, it stands for *camera obscura*, 'a darkened room'. >chamber, >comrade.

Camouflage
C20th. f. It. *camuffare* 'disguise'; perhaps associated with *camouflet* 'whiff of smoke'.

Camp
C16th. f. L. *campus* 'field'. The meaning, C20th., 'effeminate' or 'homosexual', or 'consciously artificial', has obscure origins, though there are far-fetched attempts on the Internet to find one.

Canary
C16th. What have dogs got to with canaries? The bird comes from the Canary Islands, which are named after *Canaria Insula*, which is L. for 'Isle of Dogs'. The L. word for 'dog' is *canis*, f. which we get 'canine', C17th.

Cancer
C17th. for the disease. For the zodiacal sign, C14th. f. L. *cancer*, crab, after Gk. *karkinos* from which we get 'carcinoma', C18th.

Candid
C17th. f. L. *candere* 'white', 'glistening'. Related to . . .

Candle
OE. f. the same source as above.

Canine
>Canary

Cannabis
C17th. f. Gk. *kannabis* hemp.

Canoe
C16th. f. Haitian *canoa*, through Sp.

Canter
C18th. comes f. 'Canterbury Trot', a phrase that describes the pace at which Canterbury pilgrims supposedly rode to visit the shrine of Thomas Beckett.

Capital
C13th. f. L. *caput* head.

Cappuccino
C20th. f. It. *Capuchin*. The monk's robes are the same colour as the coffee. The Capuchin monkey gets its name from the same source.

Car
C14th. Many modern things – televisions, for example – take their words from very old languages. f. L. *carra*, wagon. They are named because of the public school education, abounding in Latin and Greek, which most of their namers had experienced.

Caravan
C16th. to mean 'people travelling together'; C17th. 'covered carriage'; C20th., dangerous living quarters pulled on the backs of Volvos. f. Pers. (through Fr. *caravanne*) *karwan* 'group of desert travellers'.

Cardigan
C19th. The 7th Earl of Cardigan (1797–1868) gave his name to this garment. He also led the disastrous Charge of Light Brigade, when, in Tennyson's words, 'Into the valley of Death / Rode the six hundred'. >Nicotine, >Quisling, >Sandwich, >Wellington, and others for more eponymous words.

Caress
C17th. f. L. *carus* 'dear'.

Carnival
C16th. to mean a time of revelry before Lent, which was a time of fasting. f. L. *caro* 'flesh' and *levare* 'lightening'. So it's literally the 'ending of flesh-eating'. 'Carnage', C16th., 'carnal', C15th. and 'carnivorous', C17th. all have the same fleshy root.

Carol
C13th. f. OFr. *carola*, of doubtful origin; though maybe Late L. *choraula* is behind the word. This was the name for a flute accompanist to a choir.

Carrot
C16th. f. Gk. *karoton.*

Cash
C16th. f. OIt. *cassa*, 'cashbox', L. *capsa* 'case'.

Casino
C18th. diminutive of It. *casa* 'house', f. L. for 'cottage' or 'hut'.

Casserole
C18th. a diminutive of Middle F. *casse* 'pan', which comes f. MedL. *cattia* >pan, which is itself a diminutive of Gk. *kuathos* 'cup'.

Castle
C11th. f. L. *castrum.* An early word from the Normans. The L. can be seen in many Eng. place names, such as Chester, Colchester etc.

Castrate
C17th. f. L. *castrum* knife.

Cat
OE. While the origins of >dog are completely insecure, those of this word are less so. The original L. word was *feles*, from which we get 'feline', C17th.; but by the second millennium, the word was *cattus.* Ger. languages have variations: *Katze* in Ger. (*fur die katz* 'for the cat' is an idiom meaning 'to no purpose'). Even Fr. is in the Germanic club here with *chat.*

Catamaran
C17th. Something rare in English: a word derived f. Tamil: *katmarrum* 'tied logs'.

Cathedral
>chair

Celt
C17th f. L. *Celtoi* and earlier Gk. *Keltoi.*

Cent
C18th. US. A hundredth of a dollar. f. *centum*, L. 'hundred'. The word is everywhere in Eng.: 'percentage', 'century', 'centenarian', 'centimetre', 'centenary', 'centipede'.

Cereal
C19th. f. L. *cerealis*, concerning agriculture. f. the name of the goddess *Ceres.* Sp. and Port. get their words for >beer, *cerveza* and *cerveja,* from this root.

Certain
C12th. f. L. *certus*

Chair
C13th. f. Gk. *kathedra*, then L. *cathedra* seat, and 'cathedral' is a bishop's seat. In MedL. *cathedralis* meant 'to do with a bishop's chair'.

Chamber
C13th. f. Gk. *kamera* 'chamber'. >comrade.

Chameleon
C14th. f. Gk. *khamai* 'ground'. The creature is a 'ground-lion'.

Champagne
C17th. f. name of Eastern Fr. province where the wine is produced.

Chapel
C13th. In the C9th. St. Martin is said to have cut his cape and given half to a beggar. The cape, *capella* in L., was preserved as a relic; this word arrived C13th. It has meant: a private chapel in a house, a Nonconformist church, an association of printers and is still used today to mean a branch of a union for journalists.

Charisma
C17th. In their inevitable changes in meaning over centuries, some words decline sadly. This word is a theological term meaning the free gift of God's grace, and comes f. Gk *kharis* 'favour'. Now it is more often is used to describe what is called a 'celebrity'. >icon for a similar decline. Also >guru, >karma, >nirvana.

Chauvinism
C19th. orig. 'bellicose patriotism', f. the name of the Napoleonic veteran Nicolas Chauvin, who was always harking back to past military glories.

Chav
C20th. This word is rich is recent folk etymologies. Here are two: it comes f. 'Chatham' [or sometimes Cheltenham or Chelmsford and, for all I know, Charlton, Chingford, Chelsea, Chippenham, Charterhouse] 'average'. Or it is an acronym f. 'Council House And Violent'. I have heard it used by private school pupils in Oxford about students from the local comprehensive. In fact, it is f. a Romany word, *chavi*, 'boy'.

Checkmate
C14th. f. the Persian *sah mat*, 'The king is dead'. *Sah* is related to *tsar* and *shah*. >chess.

Cheddar
C17th. the name of the Somerset village where the cheese is produced (though versions of it are produced almost everywhere now).

Cheese
OE. comes through Germanic languages and goes back to the L. *caseus*.

Cheetah
C18th. f. a Hindi word *cita*, f. the Sanskrit *cirakaya* 'leopard'. f. *citra*, 'bright, speckled', and *kaya*, 'body'.

Chef
C19th. f. Fr. *chef de cuisine* 'head of cooking or kitchen'.

Cherry
C14th. f. Gk. *kerasos* 'cherry tree'.

Chess
C13th. f. Fr. *esches*, which came ult. f. Pers. *shah* 'king'. >checkmate.

Chicken
OE. a Germanic word. In such languages, the first sound is represented by 'k', probably reflecting an origin based imitation of the bird's cry.

Child
OE. *cild*, but the word has no other Germanic relatives, let alone relatives in other IE. languages. Fr.: *enfant* which we have in 'infant'; Swed. is *barn*, which Eng. has in the North of England and in Scotland: 'bairn'. In some dialects, the plural of child is *childer*.

Chilli
C17th. f. the Nahuatl *chilli*, through Sp. For other words f. this source, >avocado, >chocolate.

Chimpanzee
C18th. f. Angolan word *chimpanze*.

Chip
ME. exists in most Germanic languages (e.g. Du. *kip* 'beam of a plough') and in Eng., since C14th. has meant something, usually wood, cut off something larger. Under the influence of computers it has taken on a new life.

Chocolate
C17th. f. Nahuatl. For other words f. the same source >avocado, >chilli.

Chopsticks
C17th. The first part is Pidgen Eng., after *Cantonese gap* 'urgent' (familiar in the expression 'chop chop', meaning 'hurry up'). f. Cantoese *kuaizi* 'fast boys'.

Chop Suey
C19th. f. Cantonese *tsap sui*, 'odds and ends'.

Chortle
C19th. an invention of Lewis Carroll's, a combination of 'chuckle' and 'snort', from his *Through the Looking-Glass* (1872). Few of his inventions entered the language. This one and >galumph (a combination of 'gallop' and 'triumph') did. See the poem 'Jabberwocky' for the ones that didn't.

Christ
OE. f. Gk. *khristos*, a translation of Heb. 'Messiah', or 'Anointed One'. 'Christmas' is literally 'Christ's Mass'.

Chum
C17th. short for 'chamber-fellow', someone who shares rooms with you. Oxford University slang. >crony.

Church
OE. a widespread Germanic word (Ger. *Kirche*) also visible in Sc. *kirk*. ult. f. L. *kurios* 'Master', thence into Medieval Gk. in the Mass: *Kyrie Eleison* 'Lord have mercy'.

Chutney
C19th. One of many words to come into Eng. from the Indian raj. This is f. Hindi *catni*.

Chutzpah
C19th. Yid., 'unashamed self-confidence, bordering on impudence'. A young man murders his parents and then pleads for clemency because he is an orphan. That's *chutzpah*.

Ciabatta
C20th. f. It. 'slipper', presumably from the shape of the loaf.

-cide
This L. suffix is f. *cida* 'killer'. Thus 'homicide', C14th, is 'the killing of another human being' (L. *homo* 'man'); 'genocide', C20th 'the killing of a race or nation' (a mixed word etymologically, as so often in C20th. inventions f. the classical languages: *genos* is Gk. 'race'); 'regicide', C15th., 'the killing of a king' (L. *rex*).

Cider
C14th. f. Hebrew *shekhar* 'strong drink'. It went into Gk. as *sikera* and L. as *sicera*. Then it came into Eng. through OFr. *sidre*, its meaning becoming 'drink made from apples'. Ayto says that John Wycliffe translated Lk. 1.15 'He shall not drink wine or cider', which conjures up a wonderful image of Strongbow in C1st. Palestine.

Cinema
C20th. f. Gk. 'move'; hence, of course, 'movie'.

Cinnamon
C15th. of Semitic origin (Heb. *kinnamon*) then Gk. *cinnamon* and L. *cinnamon*.

Cipher
C14th. like many words to do with calculation, f. Arab.; this one stems f. *sifr* >zero.

Circum-
This prefix is L. *circus* and denotes roundness.

City
C13th. f. L. *civis* 'citizen'.

Clan
C14th. The Gael. is *clann*, 'offspring' etc., but ultimately the word goes back, through OIr. *cland*, to L. *planta*, sprout.

Claret
C14th. f. L. *clarus* 'clear'. Modern Fr. still has *clairet* 'pale wine'. But by C17th., when most red wine imported came from Bordeaux, the word came to mean 'red Bordeaux'.

Claustrophobia
>phobia

Cleave
There are two distinct words, both OE., and, curiously, one means to separate: for example, to 'cleave' a piece of wood is to separate it into two (hence 'cleavage' and 'cleaver'); while the other means to stick together: on marriage in the *Book of Common Prayer*, we are told that a man will 'cleave unto his wife'. This is a coincidence. The first 'cleave' goes back to one old IE. base, and is linked to our 'carve'. The second also goes back to a different IE. base, for 'stick', from which we get 'glue'. Bryson has a list of words in English that mean two virtually opposite things. They include 'fast' ('stuck hard' or 'dashing along'), 'sanction' ('allowed' or 'prevented') and 'bolt' ('lock up' or 'dash away'). Such words are called contronyms. Mostly they are derived from different words, and the resemblance is coincidental.

Cliché
C19th. This word for 'hackneyed phrase' comes f. printing. It was imit. of the sound of metals meeting: so a word was a cliché – it had been printed many times before.

Cliff
C12th. a Germanic word of unknown origin. ModGer. is *Klippe* 'crag'.

Climax
C14th. to mean 'ascending series', but by C18th. meant the goal itself. So are words always changing their meaning. f. Gk. *klimax* 'ladder'.

Clink
C19th. slang term for 'prison'. It was the name of an actual prison in Southwark, London.

Clique
C18th. f. Dutch *klikken*.

Clock
C14th. a Germanic word, which ModGer. has in *Glocke* 'bell'. f. MedL. *clokka* 'bell'. >bell.

Clown
C16th. perhaps of LG. origin; Frisian, many believe, is a very close relative of Eng.: *klonne* 'clumsy man'.

Club
For both the heavy stick, C13th. and the association of people, C17th., f. ON. *klubba*.

Co-, com-, con-
This L. prefix denotes 'jointly', 'with'. Some examples are 'cohere', C16th., (L. *herare* 'stick'); 'coition', C17th., (*ire* 'go'; 'collaborate'. C19th. (*labor*); 'coincide', C18th., *incidere* 'fall'; 'compact', C14th., (*pangere*, 'fasten'); 'concubine', C13th., (*cub-*, lie down, as in 'cubicle'); 'confer', C16th. (*ferre* 'bring'). >companion.

Coax
C16th. Orig. to fool someone; current meaning a century later. Origin unknown.

Cock
OE. male domestic fowl. C14th., male bird, perhaps imit. Compare Ger., where the cry is *kikeriki* and Fr., *coquerico* (and the creature is *coq*). The meaning, C17th., 'penis' is obscure in origin. The word is not used, even for the bird, in 'polite society' in the US, where 'rooster' is preferred. >titbit.

Cockney
C14th., f. *cokeney*, 'a cock's egg'. orig., 'pampered child' and, by extension, 'an effeminate man'; one, I suppose, 'tied to his mother's apron strings'. C16th., a townsman, born in London; specifically, one born within the sound of Bow Bells, therefore an Eastender. Jonathon Green (1996) quotes

a story from John Minsheu's *Ductor in Linguas* (1617). I have modernized the spelling: 'A citizens's son riding with his father out of London into the country . . . asked when he heard a horse neigh, what the horse did, his father answered, the horse doth neigh; riding farther he heard a cock crow and said doth a cock neigh too?' A lovely folk etymology. The meanings all cohere in the countryman's assumption that townees are ineffective.

Cockroach
C17th. f. Sp. *cucaracha*.

Cocksure
C16th. Simply to be 'as sure as a cock'. Here is Lord Melbourne, Victorian statesman, to the notoriously opinionated Lord Macaulay (who, according to legend, was the last Englishman to have read every important book): 'I wish I could be as cocksure about one thing as you are about everything'.

Coconut
C17th. Port. traders jocosely applied *coco* 'grinning face' to the nut they found on the subcontinent.

Cod
C13th. of unknown origin. Ayto writes that most fish names are obscure in their etymologies. >eel.

Coffee
C17th. f. Arab. *qahwah* 'coffee' and, earlier 'wine'; or possibly f. a place name *Kaffa* when the crop was grown. The word might have come to Eng. through It. *caffe* or Du. *koffie*.

Cognac
C16th. f. the name of a Fr. town in Charente.

Coleslaw
C18th. f. Du. *kool* 'cabbage' and *sla* 'salad'.

Colleen
C19th. f. Irish *caile* 'country girl or woman'.

Colour
C13th. f. L. *color*, which has an underlying meaning 'hide'; the verb is *celere*.

Comb
OE. has been traced to an IE. word from which Sanskr. and Gk. respectively get *jambhas* and *gomphos*, both 'tooth'. ModGer. is *Kamme*. It is there in various forms in nearly all European languages.

Comedy
C14th. f. Gk. *komos* 'revel', then L. and OFr. *comedie*.

Companion
C13th. f. L. *com* and *panes* 'bread'. Hence someone you share a meal with.

Comrade
C16th. not one of those >co- words, but f. Sp. *camarada* room-mate, descending f. >*camera*, 'room'.

Concubine
>co-.

Condom
C18th. A folk etymology tells us the condom was the invention of a Dr Condom, but it wasn't. It's more likely, though this is by no means certain, that it comes f. It. *guantone*, 'little glove'.

Cook
OE. An IE. root led to L. *coquus*, whence Eng. got its noun (the verb followed later). The IE. is visible in other branches of the family. It is also (surprisingly as it might seem) in 'biscuit' (>bi-). 'Cookie', C18th., despite appearances, is unrelated, and comes f. Du. *koek* 'cake'.

Corduroy
C18th. A folk etymology says that this is f. Fr. *corde du roi* 'king's cord'; in fact the likely derivation is, as often, duller. *Cord* denoted 'ribbed fabric', and *duroy* is an obsolete word for coarse cloth.

Coriander
C14th. f. Gk. *koriandrom*. Both Webster and Hitchings say that the Greeks named it after *koris* 'bedbug', which the leaves smelt like, but *Chambers* doesn't mention this, and I haven't knowingly smelt any bedbugs.

Cork
C14th. f. Arab., the word went into Sp. *alquarque* (note the Arab. definite article here: >Allah, >alcohol and others) to mean 'cork-soled shoe'.

Cormorant
C13th. f. MedL. *corvus marinus* 'sea raven'.

Corpse
>body

Cot
C17th. 'light bed', then C19th. 'child's bed'. f. Hindi *khat* 'couch' etc. f. Sanskr. *khatva*.

Country
C13th. Go back into L. and you find a phrase *terra contrata* 'land opposite'. The second part of the phrase assumed a life of its own, and comes to us through OFr. The phrase 'country dancing' may be obscene.

Certainly 'country matters' in *Hamlet* 3:2, where the prince teases Ophelia unkindly, is.

Courage
C13th., but with modern meaning C14th. f. L. *cor* 'heart' (seen by Romans, as by us, at least metaphorically, as the seat of all feelings).

Cousin
C13th. f. L. *consorbious.* The second part comes f. *soror* 'sister'.

Covenant
C13th. this word for 'agreement', especially between God and his people, comes f. L. *con* 'with' and *venire* 'come'. By C14th., it had its legal usage.

Cow
OE. *cu.* a widespread Germanic word with an IE. root which appears in L. *bos*, Gk. *bous*, whence comes our 'bovine', C19th.

Cowslip
OE. f. *cu* + *slyppe* 'slimy stuff'; so it was a plant that grew among cowpats.

Crab
OE. A widespread Germanic word. ModGer. is *Krebs.*

Crag
C13th. of Celtic origin. OIr. is *crekk.*

Crap
C20th. One of the most enduring (and arguably endearing) folk mythologies is that this word comes from the name of Thomas Crapper (1837–1910), who was indeed a pioneering manufacturer of sanitary equipment: but he was only nine years old when the word was first recorded in print to mean 'defecate'; ult. from the Du. *krappe.*

Crapulous
C16th. Nothing to do with the above. f. L. and earlier Gk. *kraepale*, in modern terms 'hangover'. When people say that they 'feel like crap' after a heavy night, the two origins are coming together.

Cravat
C17th. This now rather caddish neckwear comes (through Fr.) f. Serbo-Croat *hrvat.*

Crawl
C14th. unknown origin, though Old Icelandic has *kraffla.*

Create
C15th. f. L. *creare* 'produce'.

Crèche
C19th. f. Fr. 'manger'.

Creed
C12th. f. L. *credo*, the first word in the Mass 'I believe'. f. *credulus* 'ready to believe'. from which Eng. gets 'credible', C14th.

Cretin
C18th. The strange story is something like this. It's f. a Swiss-French dialect word *crestin* 'Christian' used to refer to mentally handicapped people, not disparagingly to the people or to Christianity, but to suggest they were as human as any Christian.

Cricket
C16th., the game; origin obscure. Some offer Fr. *criquet*, 'wicket', but this seems circular and unlikely for the most English of all games.

Crimson
C14th. f. Arab. *kirmizi*. The word came into Eng. through MedL. *cremesinus*.

Crisis
C15th. f. Gk. *krisis* 'turning point of a disease'. The wider meaning arrived C17th.

Criss-cross
By C19th. this had come to its present meaning. But it comes ult. from early modern Eng. *c(h)risse-crosse*: the crucified figure was depicted at the front of school primers etc. The significance of the first part of the word is now lost.

Crocodile
C13th. f. Gk. *kroke* 'pebble' + *drilos* 'worm'.

Crocus
C17th. f. Gk. *krokus*; prob. of Semitic origin. It's in Heb. *karkom* and Arab. *kurkum*.

Croissant
C19th. Fr. for 'crescent'. The shape is the deciding factor here, as with >bagel.

Crony
C17th. Cambridge University slang f. Gk. *khronius* 'long-lasting'. Cronies are old mates, probably originating from the same public school. The word was at first non-pejorative. >chum for an example of Oxford University slang.

Cross
OE. f. L *crux*, orig. through OIr. *cros*.

Cuckoo
C13th. f. OFr. *cucu*. It. is *cucu*. Ger. is *Kuckuck*, Du. is *koekkoek*; imit., obviously.

Cul-de-sac
C19th. Fr. 'bottom of the sack.'

Cunt
C13th. There was in Oxford, Ayto tells us, a street called Gropecuntlane in early medieval times. Chaucer uses a form of it, *queynte*, in both *The Miller's Tale* and *The Wife of Bath's Tale*. This makes a point about taboo words: their degrees of taboo-ness vary from century to century. While not exactly respectable in 1350, this one was usable. Not quite respectable, though: it is, says Hughes, 'a likely speculation' that Norman Fr. 'count' was replaced by the Germanic 'earl' because the Fr. sounded like this word. The word is still (but for how much longer?) largely taboo.

Currant
C16th. This fruit was orig. exported from Corinth, and the name is an Eng. version of Anglo-Norman *raisin de corauntz*, 'grape from Corinth'. Johnson said it should be spelt 'corinth'.

Curry
C16th. f. Tamil *kari*, 'relish with rice'.

Cushy
C20th. In his poem 'The Chances', Wilfred Owen has a cockney soldier musing on his chances in the forthcoming battle. Two of them are 'wounded – bad or cushy', and presumably he thinks, if he thinks about it all, that the word comes f. 'cushion'. But it comes f. the Hindi *khush* 'pleasant'; orig. Pers.

Cycle
>bicycle

Cynic
C16th. f. Gk *kuon* >dog.

Czar
C16th. Russian, adapted f. L. *Caesar*. So is 'kaiser'.

D

Dachshund
C19th. Ger. 'badger-dog'. The creature was bred to get down setts.

Dad, dada, daddy
C16th., imit. of baby's sounds, it is there in Sansk. *tata* and Gk. *tata*. Cf. mama, papa, baba etc.; and something like this is prob. in languages everywhere.

Daffodil
C16th. f. L. *affodillus*. It's a plant related to the asphodel, and the 's' may have been lost because in Medieval printing 's' looked like 'f'. Where the initial 'd' came from is unknown.

Dahlia
C18th. f. the C18th. Swedish botanist's name, Andreas Dahl.

Dairy
C13th. a Germanic word with an IE. root that meant 'servant woman', especially one who made bread, Gothic *deigan* = 'bread'. The move from 'bread' to 'milk' is left unexplained in *Chambers*, *SOED* and *Webster*.

Daisy
f. OE. *daeges eage* 'day's eye'. The flower covers its yellow disc in the evening and uncovers it in the morning. This sounds like a folk etymology, like >butterfly and >marmalade and others, but it isn't.

Damage
>damn

Dame
C13th. f. L. *domina*, fem. form of *dominus* Lord.

Damn
C13th. f. L. *damnus* 'loss', whence also 'damage', C14th.

Dance
C13th. Although the word is widespread in Europe, in Rom. languages, Germanic ones and even Russian, its origins are obscure.

Dandelion

C15th. f. Fr. *deni-de-lion*, lion's teeth. Though this sounds like a folk etymology, unlike >butterfly and >marmalade and many others, it isn't.

Dandy

C18th. orig. Sc., and maybe a diminutive of the name 'Andrew'.

Dark

OE. a Germanic word, though there is an OIr. word *derg* 'red', so there may be an IE. base.

Date

C13th. the fruit name is f. L. *dactylus*, ult. f. Gk. *daktulos* 'toe'. The meaning to do with time, C14th. is f. L. *Data Romae* 'given at Rome', a formula used in dating letters.

Daughter

OE. widespread among all IE. languages, except for Rom. and Celt. (*filia* L. and *merch* Welsh respectively). ModGer. has *Tochter* – a 'sisterhood of man' word: its source is somewhere in the Crimea. See Introduction.

Dawn

C15th. a back-formation f. 'dawning', ME. The word stems f. OE. *dagung* 'daying'. As a given name, it is an invention of sentimental novelists, early C20th., much as 'Wendy' was an invention by the playwright, J M Barrie, and 'Fiona' (Gael. *fionn* 'white girl') by the novelist, Walter Scott.

Day

OE. *daeg*. f. a prehistoric Germanic source (Ger. *Tag*).

De–

This L. prefix denotes 'down, away from'. Examples are: 'debauch', C16th. (the second part has unknown origin); 'decamp', C18th.; (simply 'leave the camp'); 'decapitate', C17th., (L. *caput* 'head'); 'defy', C14th., (*fides* 'faith').

Dead

OE. a Germanic word, ON. *deyja* = 'die' and ModGer. is *tot*.

Decade

C15th. ult. f. Gk. *deka* 'ten'. 'Decalogue', C14th., (*logos* 'saying') = The Ten Commandments.

Deci–

This L. prefix denotes 'ten'. Some exmples: 'decimate', C17th., 'punish soldiers by executing one in ten'. The word has largely lost this meaning, and only the pedantic still stand up for it. Indeed, the sense of 'wholesale slaughter' was present in C16th. 'Decimal', C16th., is from the same source.

Deer
OE. orig. meant any animal, usually four-legged, as opposed to a two-legged one, or a human being. It still does in Ger. *Tier* and in other Germanic languages. In *King Lear*, Shakespeare has Edgar sing an old song (3:4) with the line 'mice and rats and such small deer'. A Germanic word with an IE. root that meant 'breathing creature'. >Venison also had a general meaning orig.

Default
C13th. f. ME. *faut*, stemming f. L. *fallere*, 'fail' + *de-*. This is one of a group of words for which the meaning has widened in the last twenty years under the influence of computers. Orig., it meant 'an imperfection', or 'a failure to act'. Now, it means what happens when you do nothing, as in 'default mode'.

Defenestrate
C17th. The root is obvious, in the OFr. *fenetre*, 'window'. It goes back to Latin. *de-* is 'out of'. L. is *fenestra*, whence it came f. a neighbouring non-IE. language. So, to chuck something or someone out of a window. I am sure that it once was, in Portugal, a means of political assassination. Jan Masaryk, the Czech foreign minister, was claimed to have been defenestrated by the communists in 1948. It was also a method for commtting suicide there.

Dekko
C19th. Br. Army. 'To have a quick look at something': the word was picked up f. Hindi *dekhna* 'to see'.

Delicious
C12th. ult. f. L. *delicere* 'entice', as is 'delight', C13th.

Delta
C16th. The name of the V shape at the end of rivers – see the mouth of the Nile, for example. f. the shape of *delta*, fourth letter of the Gk. alphabet.

Demi-
This Fr. prefix, ult. f. L. *dimidius*, denotes 'half'. Examples are 'demi-monde', C19th., 'world inhabited by people of half-respectable and half-bohemian types'; and 'demigod', 'creature half-god and half-man'.

Democracy
C16th. This slippery word comes f. Gk. *demos* 'people'; is found in late L., *democratia*. *−cracy* signifies 'rule': 'plutocracy', C17th., (Gk. *ploutus* 'wealth') is the rule of the rich; 'autocracy', C17th. (Gk. *autos* 'self') is the rule of

one person. In Gk. democracy neither women nor slaves had the vote. For a (presumably) exhaustive list of '-cracy' words, see Hellweg.

Demon
C15th. The word could mean any of the following: 'evil sprit', 'inferior divinity', 'genius', 'attendant spirit'. Philip Pullman, in his novel sequence *His Dark Materials*, uses it resonantly in the third sense; ult. f. Gk. *daimon*, through L.

Denim
C17th. f. Fr. *de Nimes*, a town in S France where *serge de Nimes* was produced.

Derby
C18th. The Early of Derby founded the race in 1780. The term was later used for any sporting event, and the current use to mean a match between local rivals is C20th; so now, 'local derby' is a tautology.

Dervish
C16th. f. Pers. *darvis* 'poor'. So, 'religious beggar'. They didn't all whirl.

Devil
OE. f. Gk. *diabolos*. It came from a verb which originally meant 'slander'.

Dhal
C20th. f. Hindi. *dal* 'lentil'.

Dharma
probably C20th. f. Sanskr. It means 'ideal truth' in Buddhism; 'moral law or behaviour' in Hinduism.

Diary
C16th. f. L. *diarium* 'daily allowance', in ME.; L., 'journal'.

Die
C12th. prob. f. ON. *deya*. There may be an IE. base that also led to Gk. *thanatos* 'dead'.

Diesel
C19th. the name of the inventor Rudolf Diesel (1858–1913).

Dilly-dally
C17th. one of those playful hyphenated words that pepper Eng. It's formed f. 'dally' (origin unknown). Others are >arty-farty, >namby-pamby and >shilly-shally.

Dinghy
C19th. f. Hindi *dingi*.

Diplodocus
C19th. The first part is f. Gk. for 'double'. It was believed that this immensely long dinosaur had a supplementary brain in its tail, hence 'two-brained'. The last part of the word is f. Gk. for 'beam'.

Dipsomania
C19th.f. Gk. *dipso* 'thirst' and *mania*.

Dirt
C13th., f. earlier *drit*. 'unclean matter'; C17th., 'soil'.

Dis-
This L. prefix denotes 'reversal', 'negation' or 'lack'. Some examples: 'discomfort', C14th.; 'disconnect', C20th.; 'disgrace', C16th.; 'dislike', C16th.

Dish
OE. f. L. *discus*.

Dismal
C13th. f. L. *dies* 'day' and *mali* 'evil'.

Dismay
C13th.; nothing to do with the above. f. *dis-* 'without' and a Germanic base *mag* 'power'. To dismay someone was orig. to take power away from them. The last part of the word is the same as the verb 'may'.

Distil
C14th. f. L. *de-* 'down' and *stillare* 'drop'.

Doctor
C14th. f. L. *docere* 'teach'. There were doctors of religion and philosophy etc. before the word took on its usual modern meaning in C16th.

Dodo
C17th. f. Port. *doudo* 'fool', and applied to the bird because it was clumsy.

Doff
>don

Dog
Late OE. *docga*. Nobody knows where the word comes from. Until C16th. the usual word in Eng. was 'hound'. No other European language has anything like 'dog'. After a few centuries, Germans borrowed the word, but only to mean a particular kind of hound: *dogge*, for example, meant 'large dog, or mastiff', and Swed. has 'dogg', also 'mastiff'. Did the word 'leap up', dog-like, from a local dialect?

Doggerel
C14th. f. ME *doggerel* 'worthless', today: 'bad verse'. 'Dog Latin' is bad L., and this word may be related to that, and to the previous word.

Dolphin
C13th. f. Gk. *delphis.*

Dominion
C15th. f. L. *dominus* 'lord', as are 'dominant', C15th., and 'dominate', C17th.

Domino
C19th. f. the It. cry *Domino!* 'Master!' (see above) presumably shouted at the end of a game.

Don
C14th. In the sense of 'put on', a contraction of 'do on'. 'Doff', also C14th., is a contraction of 'do off'. To mean academic, C17th., f. L. *dominus* 'Lord', *via* the Sp. gentleman's title.

Doner
C20th. f. Turk. *kabab* 'rotating'.

Donkey
C18th. origin obscure; pronounced 'dunkey', there are two possible origins: 'dun', the colour, and the name 'Duncan'.

Dope
C19th. US. meaning 'lubricating fluid', then 'narcotic', then 'dimwit', then 'illicit information'. f. Du. *doop* 'thick sauce'.

Dormouse
C15th. of origin unknown, though perhaps the creature got its name by being 'dormant'. Lewis Carroll had this possibility in mind when he wrote about his 'Dormouse . . . fast asleep' in *Alice's Adventures in Wonderland.*

Doubt
C13th. f. L. *dubius.*

Dough
OE. a widespread Germanic word with (unsurprisingly for 'the staff of life') IE. roots that also travelled into Gk., Sanskr. and L. The meaning 'money' is C19th.

Dove
C12th. a Germanic word. OS. is *duba*, and ModGer. is *Taube.*

Dragon
C13th. f. L. *draco*, ult. Gk. *drakon.* There is a connection with the verb *drakein* 'see': perhaps the creature stared into you.

Dram
C16th. The word for a small amount of [usually] >whisk(e)y comes from the same root as *drachma*, the now obsolete Gk. coin, and means

'handful'. The word is there in United Arab Emirates currency: *dirham*, C18th.

Drama
C17th. f. Gk.

Drive
OE. a word with no cognates outside the Germanic group, but within which it is widespread; OHG. is *triban*.

Dromedary
C14th. Interesting because of its (unlikely on the face of it) connection with >aerodrome, >syndrome, >palindrome. The Gk. *dromas* is 'runner' and the animal gets the name from its speed.

Drug
C14th. of unknown origin; OFr. is *drogge*, and it has spread over Europe.

Druid
C16th. Celt., of course, but arrived through L. *druides*. Its origin is disputed: it may be in Celt. *derw* 'true' or in a base meaning 'tree', f. which Irish gets *daur* 'oak' and Eng. gets 'tree' itself.

Drum
C16th. f. LG. *trommel* 'drum'. ModGer. still has this word.

Dude
C19th. US. origin unknown, but maybe f. Ger. dialect *dude* 'fool'.

Dumb-bell
C18th. f. a Germanic word of unknown origin + bell. It's a bell with no clapper.

Dunce
C16th. Duns Scotus (d. 1308) was a theologian whose ideas went out of fashion. The saying was *Duns men, Dunces disciples.*

Dungaree
C18th. f. Hindi *dungri*.

Dyslexia
C20th. f. Gk. *dus* 'not' and *lexis* 'word'.

E

Eagle

C14th. f. L *aquila*, which may be related to *aquilius* 'dark brown'. from this word, of course, we get 'aquiline', usually applied to a nose the shape of an eagle's beak. Before the word came to us through Fr., the Eng. word was *erne*, f. OE *earn*, which survives in 'sea-erne'.

Ear

OE. *eare*. The word, as one might expect for something so basic, goes back to an IE. base, and is present in most European languages: Fr. *oreille*, Ir. *o*, and Sp *orecha*.

Early

OE. f. a root which survives in the archaic 'ere', meaning 'before'. There is an IE. root: Gk. has *eri*.

Earth

OE. has an IE. base, and its cousins include *erde*, *aarde* (>aardvark) and *jord* (Ger., Du., Swed. & Danish respectively). It's in all the Germanic languages, while most Rom. languages have a L. root *terra*, from which Eng. gets >terrestrial and >Mediterranean.

Earwig

OE. Someone told me when I was a child that these creatures would wiggle inside my >ear, and I believed them. The Anglo-Saxons (hence *earwicga*), the French (*perce-oreille* – lit. 'pierce-ear') and the Germans (*ohrwurm* – 'ear-worm') believed that too. It isn't true, though.

Easel

C17th. f. Dutch *ezel* 'ass', f. L. *asinus*. Simlarly, Fr. *chevalet* 'easel' had an earlier meaning, 'little horse'.

East

OE. has an IE. root and is in all Germanic languages. The name of the goddess of the sun rising was a related word *Austron*. In OE. her name was *Eastre* from which we get . . .

Easter
OE. The historian Bede derived the word from the goddess named above.

Eat
OE. a widespread Germanic word f. an IE. root.

Eavesdrop
C15th. The OE. is *yfesdrype*, 'water dropping from the eaves'. The 'eave' was, and still is, a sloping part of the roof. If you waited to hear the drops fall, you were an eavesdropper.

Echo
C14th. f. Gk. word for 'sound', which developed into the name of the mythological nymph *Echo* who faded slowly of unrequited love until only her voice was left. Ovid writes about her in *Metamorphoses*: 'Echo . . . cannot speak unless someone else has spoken . . .'

Ecology
C19th. f. Gk. *oikos* 'house' (used here to mean the environment). *Logy* is f. Gk. 'to study', as in 'anthropology' etc.

Economy
C16th. f. Gk. *oikos* 'house' and *nemein* 'manage'.

Ecstacy
C14th. Gk. *ekstasis* signifies 'being out of it', 'out of your mind', and the word comes to us through L. and OFr.

Eczema
C18th. f. Gk. *ek* 'out' and *zein* 'boil'. The IE. base turns up in our >yeast.

Eden
C14th. f. Heb. *edhen* 'delight'.

Edge
OE. a Germanic word with an IE. root, present in ModGer. *Ecke* 'corner'. By C16th., it meant 'incite'. That's where 'egg on' comes from: nothing to do with what a bird lays.

Educate
C15th. f. L. *e-* 'out' and *ducere* 'lead'. So 'education' isn't telling people things, but helping them to draw those things out from themselves.

Eel
C13th. Though it has relatives, such as Modern Du. *aal*, it is of obscure origin; >cod. Ely in Cambridgeshire is etymologically 'the place where the eels are'. For much fun with all this, see Graham Swift's novel *Waterland*.

Eerie
C13th. Orig. 'fearful' but by C18th. had come to mean 'uncanny'. Origin obscure, but OE *earg* = 'cowardly'.

Effeminate
C14th. f. L. *ef-* 'from' and *femina* 'woman'. Nothing to do with (though often confused with) . . .

Effete
C17th. This word stems f. L. for 'from', + >*foetus*. The word means 'weak', as a woman feels after giving birth.

Egg
C14th. The noun goes back, unsurprisingly, to an IE. base signifying 'bird'. Then Sansk. gets *vis* and L. *avis* (whence Eng. gets 'aviary' and 'ovary'). The word turns up, in different forms, everywhere in the family of languages: It. *uovo*, Fr. *oeuf*. For the unrelated usage 'egg on' >edge.

Ego
C18th. L. for 'I'. Thus an 'egotist', C18th., is very aware of him/herself. Freud (C20th.) made the word virtually indispensable. For him, the word meant 'conscious part of the mind' as opposed to >id and >libido.

Eid
C20th. The festival marks the end of Ramadan. The name comes f. Arabic *id ul fitre* 'end of fast-breaking'.

Eight
OE. The origin of this word is traceable everywhere in the IE. family. L. is *octo*, and it is there in Fr. *huit* and in other Rom. languages. All the words for numbers have histories like this.

Eisteddfod
C19th. f. Welsh *eistedd* 'sit', f. an IE. root.

Elbow
OE. f. a Germanic word that meant 'arm-bend'. OE. was *eln* = 'length of forearm' + *boga* = 'bow'. Modern Du. is *elleboog*. So, an elbow 'makes a bow of the arm'.

Electricity
C17th. f. Gk. *elektron* 'amber'. The Greeks had found out that if you rub amber it will draw particles to itself, so the word seemed right when electricity was first explored.

Elephant
C13th. f. Gk. *elephas* 'ivory', through L. and Rom. When the word first came into OE. as *olfend* it meant camel: not much of either creature was known in N. Europe at this time.

Eloquent
C14th. f. L. *e*- 'out' + *loqui* 'speak'.

Embarrass
C17th. This may be f. Port. *embaracar*, which means 'halter'; or it may be f. It. *imbarrare* 'surround with bars': vulgar L. had *barra* 'bar'.

Embonpoint
C18th. Readers of James Joyce's *Ulysses* will be familiar with this word, where it is used salaciously to mean 'a woman's bust'. f. Fr. *en bon point* 'in good condition'.

Embrace
C14th. f. L. *in* and *brachium* 'arm'.

Embryo
C16th. f. Gk. *embruon*. *Em*- = 'in', *bruein* 'swell'.

Emerald
C13th. f. Gk. *smaragdos* through L. and Rom. The Semitic root *baraq* meant 'shine', and Heb. is *bareqet*.

Emir
C17th. f. Arab. *amara* 'command'.

Emperor
C13th. f. L. *imperare* 'command'. Thus, of course, 'empire', also C13th., and 'imperial', C14th.

Emu
C17th. f. Port. *ema* 'ostrich'; also applied formerly to cassowaries and rheas.

Encore
C18th. f. Fr. 'again'. But not used in France as a shout at the opera, much as (according to Bryson) *nom de plume* and *bon viveur* aren't used in the way Eng. uses them.

End
OE. An IE. word is present in the Germanic: Ger. is *Ende*. L. is *ante* 'before' and Sanskr. *antas*.

Enemy
C13th. f. L. *i*- 'not' + *amicus* 'friend'.

Energy
C16th. f. Gk. *en*- + *ergon* 'work'. It goes back to IE. root which gives Eng. 'work' and 'organ'.

Enervate
C17th. Sounds like the above, and is almost an opposite. Here the prefix *e-* is L. and a negative, and *nervus* is sinew. To be enervated is to be strengthless.

England, English
OE. The Angles were a tribe from an area south of modern Denmark and north of modern Hanover. They had named their area *Angul* (Eng. 'angle') after a fishhook, because of supposed resemblance in shape of the area to the thing. They arrived in Britain in C5th. and C6th. By C8th, all the Germanic tribes in Britain were called *gens anglorum*, 'race of Angles'. Hence 'England'. A famous pun goes as follows: St Gregory (*c.*540–604) saw blond children in Rome. 'What are they?' he asked. '*Angli*' was the reply. '*Non Angli*' he replied '*sed angeli*' ('Not Angles but angels'). Adapted here from Bede.

Enigma
C17th. f. Gk. *ainissesthai* 'to speak in riddles'.

Enjoy
C14th. f. OFr. *enjoir.*

Epi-
This Gk. preposition can mean 'among', 'above' or 'upon', 'in addition to'. Thus 'epidemic', C17th., is 'among the people' (people: *demos*); 'epicentre', C19th., is 'above the centre' (*kentron*, centre); 'epitaph', C14th., is 'above the tomb' (*taphos*); 'epigraph', C17th., is 'above the writing' (*graphos*).

Epicene
C15th. f. Gk. *epikoino*, 'common to many'; so, having both male and female characteristics.

Epicure
C16th. f. the name of the Gk. philosopher *Epikouros c.*300 BC.

Equestrian, Equine
C17th. f. L. *equus* 'horse'.

Era
C18th. The plural of L. *aera* 'copper counters'.

Ersatz
C19th., as in 'ersatz jewellery'. f. Ger. *Ersetzen* 'replace'.

Esquimau
C16th. A North American word meaning 'eaters of raw flesh'.

Esperanto
C19th. The inventor of the language L L Zamenhof gave it this name to mean 'One who hopes'.

Etymology
C14th. f. Gk. *etymon* 'true sense of a word'. >logy. See Introduction for my notes on 'the etymological fallacy'.

Eucharist
C14th. f. Gk. *eukharistia* 'thanksgiving'. The middle part is in *kharis* 'favour, grace'. >charisma.

Eunuch
C15th. f. Gk. *eune* 'bed' and *ekhein* 'guard'. Thus, 'a guardian of the bedchamber'. The connection with 'castration' is easy enough to infer.

Eureka
C17th. f. Gk. *heureka* 'I have found'. Said to have been shouted by Archimedes when, while in his bath, he discovered the means of determining how much base metal there was in Hiero's golden crown. Pure gold would displace more water than adulterated gold.

European
C17th. This word of unknown origin first applied to central Greece. But Europa was an unfortunate girl raped by Jupiter in the guise of a bull.

Ever
OE. An Eng. word, known nowhere else, and of no known origin.

Evil
OE. *Yfel*. The word is in Germanic languages, and rooted in IE. *up* 'over'. The evil person is exceeding proper limits. The word has gained in its negativity and force.

Eye
OE. The word, as one might expect for something so basic, goes back to an IE. base, and is present in most European languages: for example, It. *occhio* to Slavic *oko*.

F

Fabric
C15th. f. L. *faber* 'craftsman'.

Face
C13th. f. L. *facies* 'form, appearance', and that meaning can be seen in Eng. 'façade'.

Facsimile
>fax

Fact
C16th. f. L. *facere* 'do'.

Fad
C19th. A folk eymology says that the word is an acronym: 'For A Day'. Like most acronymic derivations (>cabal) this is untrue. In fact, the word is more likely to be a shortening of 'fiddle-faddle', 'silly talk or action', which was (C18th.) *fidfad*.

Faff
C20th. This is usually given as 'orig. unkn.', but possibly a polite evasion of >fuck.

Faith
C12th. This word, as my Welsh friend writes, is *ffudd* in her first language. It goes back to an IE. root which is there in L. *fides*, and it's also there in all the Rom. languages. We have separated from the Germanic languages here: ModGer. is *Glaube*.

Fajita
C20th. f. Mexican Sp.

Fakir
C17th. This word for a Muslim or Hindu holy man is f. Arab. for 'poor'.

Fallopian
C18th. Gabriello Fallopio (1523–1562) was a canon of Modena Cathedral and an anatomist specializing in the ear, and he first described the tubes

in the female anatomy that are named after him. I suppose that it was tubes that interested him.

Family
C15th. f. L. *famulus*, orig. 'servant', a word of obscure origin. *Familia* was derived from it, to mean all the servants, and then all the persons in a household. It was C17th. before the word narrowed down to its present meaning in Eng.

Fan
C19th. is short for . . .

Fanatic
C16th. To mean 'possessed by religious frenzy', then C18th., marked by 'excessive enthusiasm'. f. L. *fanus* temple.

Fanfare
C17th. of imit. origin say some. But it may have come, through Fr., f. Sp. *fanfarron* 'braggart', with roots in Arab. *farfar* 'chatterer'.

Fanzine
C20th. Meaning a fugitive magazine produced in honour of a rock group or a football team, the word is f. the US. and dates f. late 1940s. Its roots are in >fanatic.

Farce
C16th. f. L. *farcire* 'stuff'. Comic interludes were 'stuffed' into religious plays. By modern times, we have plays entirely composed, as it were, of stuffing.

Farm
C13th. orig. meant 'payment as rent', and this meaning is seen in its L. root *firmare* 'fix'.

Fart
OE. There is an IE. root for this work, *perd*, which is probably imitative. Versions of it are in German *farzen*, Swedish *fjarta* and Welsh *rhechain*. All so-called taboo words vary in their effect down the centuries. This one is becoming relatively innocent again, but it was unsayable in 'polite society' thirty years ago.

Fascist
C20th. f. L. *fascis* 'bundle'. Mussolini's movement was a group of forces, and they took the L. symbol as theirs.

Fat
OE. a Germanic word, and the Ger. is *Fett*.

Father
OE. *faeder*. A brother/sisterhood word, it's everywhere. L. is *pater*, was still used by public schoolboys until recently. It's in OIr. *athir*. For other such words, >arse, >axe, >brother, >mother, >sister, >star >fart.

Fatwa
C20th. Arab. 'judgement passed under Islamic sharia law' – not a death sentence, as is commonly supposed.

Fauna
C18th. Fauna was the late L. goddess of living things, and the word means all the creatures of a time or place. >Flora.

Fax
C20th. is short for 'facsimile', which comes f. the L. *fac simile*, an order: 'Make a copy of that!'

Fear
C13th. a Germanic word; OHG. meant 'deceit, ambush', and ModGer. *Gefahr* = 'danger'.

Feather
OE. a widespread Germanic word (Ger. has *Feder*) with an IE. root which is visible in Gk. *pterux* 'wing'.

Feature
C14th. f. L. *factura* 'formation'.

Feeble
C12th f. L. *flere* 'weep'.

Feisty
C20th. f. a North American word for a small dog. Its origins are in ME. for 'farting dog'.

Female
C14th. f. L. *femina* 'young woman' or 'girl'. The original form was Fr. *femelle*. Association with >male gave it its present form. 'Feminine' is obviously f. the same source, which goes back to a IE. root meaning 'suckle', which is present in L. *felare*, Gk. *thesai* and Sanskr. *dhayati*, all to do with sucking.

Fen
OE. Unsurprisingly, this word, which exists in Sansk. as *panka*, 'mud', existed in various forms all over N. Europe: *fenna* for example, in OHG. There is an IE. root.

Feng-shui
C20th. f. Chinese *feng* 'wind' and *shui* 'water'.

Fenian
?C19th. f. Ir. for a legendary band of warriors, *Fianna*. The name of the political party founded in 1926, *Fianna Fail*, is literally 'Warriors of Destiny'. It has a ring that 'The Conservative and Unionist Party' lacks.

Ferret
C14th. f. L. *furo* 'thief'.

Fetish.
C17th. f. Port. *feitico* 'charm made by art'.

Fiancé, fiancée
C19th. f. L. *fidere* 'trust'.

Fiasco
C19th. I was told that this word came from the surname of an Italian opera producer whose productions were all shambles. Attractive as the story is, the word comes f. It. *fiasco* 'bottle' which we have in 'flagon' and 'flask', which is f. L. *flasco*. Evidently, *far fiasco* 'to make a bottle' was something like our 'make a balls-up'. It is uncertain why.

Fiddle
OE. This word and >violin are related etymologically. They both go back to the name of a pre-Roman goddess, *Vitula*. Her name produced, in S. Europe, *violin* etc.; in N. Europe, prehistoric German produced *fithulon*, which let to our word 'fiddle'. The modern usuage, 'to swindle', is C19th Amer.

Film
OE., to mean 'membrane', and used for the human body: 'caul', 'prepuce', 'skin'. It was adopted, C19th., for photography.

Fire
OE. *fyr*. It is basic to civilization. Du. is *vuur*, for example. Czech, a language rarely sited in this pages, has *pyr*, which is present in our 'pyromania'.

Fish
OE. As you might expect, there's an IE. root *piskos*. You can glimpse it in the Zodiacal sign Pisces, and, to take one example, in Fr. *poisson*. The northern route is there in Ger. *Fisch*, which is where our word comes from.

Flag
C16th. to mean 'hang down', origin unknown; to mean emblem: perhaps following on from the other meaning, also C16th. The plant word is also unknown, though Du. has it.

Flagon
C15th. f. L. *flasco*. >fiasco. 'Flask', C14th., is from the same source.

Flak
C20th. Fl-a-k, f. Ger. *Flieger-abwehr-kanone*; literally, an 'aircraft defence gun'.

Flamingo
C16th. f. Port. *flamengo*, f. L. *flamma* 'flame'.

Flask
>flagon

Flaunt
C16th. of unknown origin.

Flautist
C14th. f. It. *flautista* and *flauto*, 'flute'.

Flora
C18th. This is the name of the Roman goddess of flowers, and the word means all the plant life of a given time or place. >Fauna.

Flower
C13th. f. L. *flos*, which was derived f. >Flora. The OE. word was *blostm*, which gave us 'bloom' and 'blossom', but L. came through the Normans and replaced 'blossom' except in the more limited sense. Both words have the same IE. root, which we see in 'bloom'.

Flu
C19th. short for 'influenza'. The word is 'influence' is It., and was a metaphor for 'outbreak'. *Influenza di cattarro* means 'outbreak of catarhh'.

Fluke
C19th. origin unknown.

Flummery
C17th. to denote a kind of porridge. By C18th., 'nonsense', 'humbug'. This comes f. a Welsh word *llymru*, which is of unknown origin. The 'fl' in the Eng. word is an attempt to imitate Welsh 'll'.

Flunkey
C18th. origin unknown, though maybe f. Fr. *flanker* a person who stands at someone's side. Cf. Fr. *flanc* 'side' and, our Eng. 'flank'.

Fly
OE. Eng. gets this f. Germanic. It goes back to an IE. root. Also OE., the winged insect.

Fo'c's'le
C14th. as 'forecastle'. The raised deck in the bow of a ship was often castle-shaped. The modern word has become legitimized in its spelling by sailors' pronunciation.

Focus
C17th. L. for 'hearth' or 'fireplace'.

Foetus
C14th. f. L. *fetus* 'giving birth'. >effete. Related to 'fecund' and 'fertile'.

Fog
C16th. of unknown origin, though Danish has *fog* 'spray'.

Fogey
C18th. orig unknown, though Hoad relates it to an C18th. slang word *fogram* 'old-fashioned person'.

Folk
OE. Some sources go back to an IE. root, but it is safer to identify this word's earliest appearance in OE. *folc*. It is there in Du. *volk*, and other Germanic languages.

Font
OE. f. L. for >fountain.

Fontanelle
C17th. OFr. 'little spring'. Obviously related to above.

Food
OE. Unsurprisingly the word goes back to an IE. root. The Germanic root was *foth*, from which we get, among other words, >*foster*.

Fool
C13th. f. L. *follis* 'bellows'; thus later 'windbag'. Sometimes the licensed fool in the royal court carried a bellows as a comic prop, much as Ken Dodd carries his 'tickling stick'.

Foot
OE. Unsurprisingly, we can trace this word to an IE. root, seen in L. *pes*, which supplies the words for most of the IE. languages. In Eng., we can see it in 'tripod' (*tri* = three). The Germanic descendant is *fos*. For the basic Germanic word, the 'p' sound changed to 'f'.

Fop
C15th. to mean 'fool', then C17th. 'dandy'; of uncertain origin.

Fore-
The prefix, which, unusually, is OE. and not L. or Gk., means 'before in time or rank'. This includes position, as in 'forearm', C16th. Other examples: >fo'c's'le ('forecastle'), 'forefinger', C15th. 'foregoing', C15th. and 'foreground', C17th.

Foreign
C14th. L. is *foras*, 'outside'. This sense survived into ME., but by C15th, the modern meaning had ousted it. The same root is in 'forest', C13th.

Forget
OE. f. Ger. *Fergetan*. 'lose one's hold on'; frequent in Germanic languages.

Forgive
OE. *forgeban* was a calque (see p 207) of L. *perdonare*, source of our 'pardon'.

Fornication
C13th. f. L. *fornix* 'arch'. Apparently, prostitutes lived in vaulted premises. Presumably, as Bud Flannigan sang, 'underneath the arches'.

Fortnight
OE. f. *feowertiene* 'fourteen' + *niht* 'night'. 'Sennight', 'seven nights' has gradually been lost, but was in use in Shakespeare's time, as we know from the plays.

Forum
C15th. >foreign, >forest.

Fortune
C13th. f. L. *fortuna*.

Foul
OE. A Germanic word – OHG. is *ful*; with an IE. root that appears in L. *pus* and *putridus*.

Fountain
C15th. f. L. *fons* 'spring'. >font, >fontanelle.

Fox
OE. This word has relatives in Sanskrit *pucchas* 'tail'. From this, the Germans get *fuchs*, the Dutch *vos*; and we get this word. Unsurprisingly, the animal seems to have been identified in terms of its brush.

Fracas
C18th. f. Fr. *fracasser*, It. *fracassare* 'make a din'. In Fr. *fracas* is 'roar of a train'; of unknown origin.

Franc
C14th. Fr. L. *Francorum rex* 'King of the Franks', inscribed on coins.

Fratricide
>cide

Freckle
C14th. f. ON. *freknur*.

Free
OE. A word of such importance to the human race, it appears in different forms in many places. Here are a few examples: OHG. *fri*; ON.

frjals (f. a word meaning 'free-necked'); ModGer. *frei*. Eng. gets it
f. Germanic. The IE. root appears in Sankr. *priya* 'dear', which was orig.
meaning of 'free'. It is also present in Welsh *rhydd*. The Eng. 'friend',
OE., is f. the same source.

Friend
>free

Frog
OE. *frogga*. A Germanic word, related to words in Du. (*vorsch*) and other
N. European languages.

Frost
OE. a Germanic word. Modern Du. is *vorst*.

Fruit
C12th. f. L. *fructes*.

Fry
C13th. f. L. *frigere*. An IE. root also produced L. *fervere*, which Eng. has
in 'fervent'.

Fuck
C16th. Two folk etymologies: it is an acronym, 'For Unlawful Carnal
Knowledge', or 'Fornication Under Consent of the King'. Both rubbish,
of course, and lacking in the charm of other such theories. >butterfly,
>marmalade. It is prob. Scand. in origin: A Norwegian dialect has *fukka*
'copulate' and a Swedish dialect has *focka* which can also, disturbingly,
mean 'hit'.

Fungus
C16th. f. L. *fungus*.

Fustian
C12th. 'coarse cloth'; C16th., 'pretentious'. f. the name of *Fustat*, a sub-
urb of Cairo where the cloth was made.

Futon
C20th. Japanese, 'quilted roll'.

G

Gabble

C16th. f. Modern Du. *gabbelein*, imit. of the noise geese make.

Gadget

C19th. A seamen's term. Prob. the contemporary equivalent of modern 'thing-um-a-jig', or 'whatsit' or 'doings', as in 'Pass that gadget, mate'; of unknown origin.

Gael

C14th. f. Sc. *Gaidheal* and Irish *Goidel*.

Gaga

C20th. Fr., of imit. origin.

Gaffer

C16th. Footballers use this about their manager. A contraction of 'godfather'.

Galaxy

C14th. f. Gk. *gala* 'milk'. It was orig. used to refer only to The Milky Way.

Galleon

C17th. f. Sp. *galeon*.

Galore

C17th. As in the film title *Whisky Galore*; f. Irish *goleor*, 'sufficiently'.

Galumph

>chortle

Game

OE. *gamen* 'amusement'. C13th. to mean 'sport'; of unknown origin. A separate word means 'lame', C18th. and may come f. Irish *cam* 'crooked'.

Gander

C19th. meaning 'a look'; f. the resemblance between a nosey person and a peering goose. The word for the male goose, OE., is f. MLG. *ganre*.

Gang
C12th. In his poem 'Ay Waukin O', Robert Burns (1759–1796) says that 'Freedom and Whisky gang together'. Here the word means 'journey', which is the original meaning. This is a Germanic word meaning 'go'. By C17th, it meant 'collection of things carried together', and then a group of people travelling together.

Gaol
C13th. f. L. *cavea* 'cage'.

Garage
C20th. f. OFr. *garer* 'take care'.

Garden
C14th. f. prehistoric Germanic *gardon*.

Gardenia
C18th. The flower that Billie Holiday wore in her hair is named after Alexander Garden, naturalist (d. 1791); the name, presumably, is a neat coincidence.

Gargoyle
C15th. f. OF. *gargouille* 'throat'; of imit. origin. Cf. our 'gargle', C16th.

Gas
C17th. f. Du. *gas*, based on Gk. *khaos*.

Gastric
C17th. f. Gk. *gaster* 'stomach'. It travelled into L., then Fr., *gastrique*, whence it arrived in Eng. 'Gastronomy' is 'the law of the stomach' (Gk. *nomos* law).

Gate
OE. a Germanic word: Old Frisian *gat* = 'hole'.

Gay
This comes f. an Old Provence word *gai* 'happy'. It has quite a history. Here it is, potted: C13th., it meant 'excited . . . merry . . . brilliant in colour'. Then, over the centuries . . . [of a woman's clothes] . . . 'a little *too* brilliant in colour' . . . 'given to social pleasures' . . . 'a little *too* given to social pleasures' . . . 'loose, immoral' [as in 'gay dog' and 'gay Lothario'] . . . 'a prostitute' . . . 'brash' . . . and [at last, late C20th.] 'homosexual'. (Adapted from Webster).

Gazelle
C17th. f. Arab. *gazal*.

Gazump
C20th. to raise the price of a house after an agreement; origin unknown. Earlier in the century it meant 'swindle'.

Geisha
C19th. Japanese for 'accomplished person'.

Gender
f. OFr. *genre* with a L. root *gener-*; f. which come also 'general', C13th., and 'generous', C16th. Why Eng. uses Fr. *genre* and not 'kind' or 'type' when talking about art is due to an inbuilt pretentiousness.

Genocide
>cide

Gentile
C14th. f. L. *gentiles* 'of the same family'; ult. f. *gens* 'people'.

Geo–
This Gk. prefix denotes 'earth', as in many C19th. scientific terms. 'Geology', C18th., is the 'study of the earth', 'geometry', C14th., the 'measuring of earth'.

Geordie
?C17th. The name for a Tynesider derives from the name George, though anyone from Sunderland is a 'mackem'.

Gerrymander
C19th. Ayto tells the story: in 1812, Elbridge Gerry, governor of Massachusetts, made boundary changes that aided his party, the Democrats. Someone looking at the resulting map said it looked like a salamander. The editor entered etymological history with his reply: 'A gerrymander, you mean!'

Gestapo
C20th. German *Ge(heime)Sta(ats)po(lizei)*.

Get
C13th. Ult. f. an IE. root meaning 'sieze', it comes to Eng. through Germanic.

Ghastly
C14th. f. ME. *gast* 'terrify'. The 'h' was acquired later f. >ghost.

Ghost
OE. An IE. root produced ON. *geisa* 'rage', and the 'h' appeared, C15th., f. Flemish *gheest*. Presumably, a ghost is angry about something, as they often seem to be.

Giggle
C16th. imit.

Gigolo
C20th. Fr., possibly f. *gigolette* 'dancing girl'.

Gin

C18th. An abbreviation of Geneva. OF. *genevre* is derived f. the L. *juniperus*. Juniper figures largely in the flavour. That Calvinistic city in Switzerland became involved by coincidence of sound, and is guiltless of 'mother's ruin'.

Ginger

C13th. ult. f. Sanskr. *srngavera*. It went into Gk as *ziggiberis*, L. as *zingiber*, and arrived in ME., after a very circuitous journey, as *gingivere*.

Gipsy

C16th., when it was thought that Romany people originated in Egypt. The word is a shorted version of 'Egyptian'. In fact, they are of Hindu origin, and their language has been linked to a Sanskr. dialect.

Giraffe

C17th. f. Arab. *zarafa* through It. *giraffe*.

Girl

C13th. No-one knows where this comes from. It orig. meant 'child' of either sex.

Give

OE. a Germanic word: OHG. is *geban*.

Glad

OE. f. ON. *glaor* 'bright, joyful'.

Glass

OE. a Germanic word: ON. is *gler*.

Glen

C15th. a Gael. word: Irish is *gleann* and Welsh is *glyn*.

Glory

C13th. f. L. *Gloria*.

Glove

OE. f. Gothic *lofa* 'hand'.

Glutton

C13th. f. L. *gluttire* 'swallow'.

Gnu

C18th. f. a southern Bushman word (I am going to enjoy typing this) *!nu* (where the '!' represents a click). It went into Du. as *gnoe*.

Goat

A Germanic word with a root in IE., which also appears in L. *haedus* 'kid'.

God
OE. A Germanic word of uncertain origin.

Golf
C15th. of unknown origin. *Collins* says there is a folk etymology (once appropriate enough, no doubt) 'Gentlemen Only, Ladies Forbidden' and suggests a possible source in Middle Du. *colf* club. Hitchings refers to a Du. game *kolven*.

Good
OE. a Germanic word: OHG. is *guot* and ModGer. *gut*.

Goodbye
OE. This is a contraction of 'God be with thee'.

Goose
OE. A Germanic word with an IE. root that is visible in Sanskr. *hamsa* and other languages. OIr. *geis* is 'swan'.

Gooseberry
C16th. presumably f. 'goose' and 'berry', though why the goose is involved is uncertain. The meaning 'someone who is in the way of a romantic pairing' is C19th. Ayto suggests that the third person went gooseberry-picking while the couple canoodled.

Gorgonzola
C19th. f. the name of a village near Milan in Italy.

Gorilla
C19th. f. Gk *Gorrillae*, the name the Greeks gave to a supposed hairy African tribe.

Gormless
C18th. dialect, probably Scottish. *Gorm* is understanding, f. ON. 'gaumr'. So, obviously, a gormless person is a dimwit. Other words retain only their negative meaning include 'immaculate', 'inept', 'reckless' 'ruthless' and 'dishevelled'. Bryson is good on these.

Gospel
OE. *godspel* 'good news'.

Gossip
OE. This word was *godsibb*, a combination of >God and *sib* denoting spiritual affinity (*sib* meaning relative, >sibling, C20th., a revival of an OE. word); so, a godparent at baptism. By C12th., the word had come to mean a 'close relative', and by C16th., 'idle talker'. One of many words that have lost any religious meaning. >goodbye, >holiday, >charisma, among others.

Gourmet
C19th. Fr. 'wine merchant's assistant'.

Govern
C13th. f. L. *gubernare* 'guide, steer', then OFr. *gouvener*. The original spelling can be seen in US. Eng. 'gubernatorial'.

Grace
C12th. 'Prayer of blessing, thanks'; by C14th, 'pleasing quality'; then, as 'graceful', f. C16th., the modern sense emerges. The L. derivation supports the most recent meaning: *gratus* 'pleasing'.

-graph or graph-
This prefix or suffix is Gk. and usually signifies 'writing' and by extension something put down in some other way: hence 'autograph' C17th, *autos* 'self'; 'photograph', C19th *photo* 'light'; or it signifies the instrument that does the recording, as in 'telegraph' C18th., *tele* 'far'; 'pornography', C19th., *porne* 'prostitute'. Thus 'geography', C16th., *ge* 'earth'). >lexicography.

Gratis
L. f. 'freely'; thus, among others, 'gratitude', C16th.: one of its meanings was 'free gift'.

Grave
There are two unrelated words. The first, meaning 'burial place', OE., is a Germanic word. ModGer. *graben* = 'dig'. It survives in our 'engrave'. The 'weighty, important' meaning, C16th., is f. L. *gravis*. The IE. root produced Sanskr. *guru* and Gk. *barus*. The Eng. word comes through Gothic *kaurus* 'heavy'. 'Gravity', C17th., is f. the same root.

Green
OE. a Germanic word: OHG. is *gruoni*. The underlying meaning is 'colour of growing things', and 'grow' is f. the same root.

Grey
OE. A Germanic word with an IE. root. W B Yeats ('When you are old and gray . . .') and US. Eng. both prefer the older spelling.

Greyhound
OE. Greyhounds are rarely grey, apparently. The first part comes f. OE. 'bitch'. The rest is the original English word for >dog. So a homely word would be 'bitchdog'.

Gringo
C19th. an offensive Mexican word for an Anglo-American; perhaps f. Sp. *gringo* 'gibberish'; or perhaps (says Green) f. *griego* 'Greek'; so, 'foreign'.

Grog
C18th. The rum and water served out in the Royal Navy was prob. named after an admiral who ordered the dilution of the drink, and who wore a *grogram* cloak, a coarse one made of a mixture of materials.

Gross
C14th. There are two unrelated words. The first, meaning 'coarse' and the like, f. L. *grossus*; to mean, C15th., 'twelve dozen', f. Fr. *gros* 'great'.

Grumpy
C18th. a dialect word of obscure origin. Danish has *grum* 'cruel'.

Grudge
f. OFr. *grouchier*, of unknown origin.

Guerrilla
C19th., diminutive of Sp. *guerra* 'war'; thus 'little war'.

Guess
C14th. Orig. 'take aim', it's prob. f. ON., which had *geta*.

Guest
C13th. a Germanic word with an IE. root that emerges in L. *hostis* 'enemy' and Old Slavic *gosti* 'friend'.

Guffaw
C18th. prob. Sc.; presumably imit. of a loud coarse laugh.

Guilt
OE. of unknown origin, and no other language has a relative.

Guitar
C17th. f. Gk. *kithara* through Sp. *guitarra*.

Gumption
C18th. Sc., a shortening of *rumble-gumption*, of unknown origin.

Gun
C14th. f. the pet version of the Scand. female name *Gunnhildr*. Both parts of this name mean 'war', which may say a good deal about a people. A daughter called 'War-War'?

Guru
C17th. Hindu spiritual teacher, f. Sankr. *guru* 'weighty, >grave'. Now much debased, as in 'I am now seen as a guru in educational circles' (actually heard by me). Other debased religious words are >charisma, >karma, >nirvana.

Gusto
C17th. f. L. *gustus* 'taste'. It is there in Fr. *gout* 'taste' and also in Eng. 'disgusting'.

Gymnasium
C16th. f. Gk. *gumnasion*; ult. f. *gumnos* 'naked'. Gymnasts trained naked.
L. borrowed the word to mean 'school'.

Gynaecology
>queen

H

Hack, Hackney
C14th. These words have an interesting journey. Orig. 'horse for hire', by C16th., hackney meant 'drudge' and even 'prostitute'. 'For hire' is probably significant. Certainly, the shortening 'hack', C19th., suggests this, denoting as it does a writer who will write anything for money. C17th., it was short for 'hackney-carriage'. Perhaps it derives f. the name of the area in West London. The original meaning survives: taxis still have labels calling themselves 'hackney carriages'.

Haddock
C14th. origin unknown >cod.

Haemo-
Gk. 'blood'; so 'haemorrhage', C17th., (*rhegnunai* 'bursting forth'); 'haemorroid', C14th., is 'flowing with blood'.

Haggis
C15th. Origin unknown, though Webster suggests an earlier word *haggen* 'chop'; Ayto mentions this possibility, but suggests the OFr. *agace* 'magpie', which was also used for 'pie', and a haggis is collection of all sorts of meat, much as the bird's nest is full of odds and ends.

Ha-ha
C17th. 'sunk fence or wall'. In Trollope's *Barchester Towers*, whether you are one side or the other of this at the Thornes' *fete champetre* determined whether you were 'quality' or 'non-quality'. Prob. named after the merry laughter occasioned when your friend encountered it unexpectedly.

Hair
OE. a Germanic word of unknown origin. ModGer. has *haar*.

Hadj
C18th. f. Arab. *hajj* 'pilgrimage'.

Halal
C20th. Arab. 'lawful'.

Halibut

C15th. a Germanic word (LG. has *higglibut*) f. *haly* 'holy' and *butte* 'flat fish': it was eaten on holy days only.

Halitosis

C19th. f. L. *halitus* 'breath'.

Hall

OE. a Germanic word. Du. has *hal*.

Hallelujah

C16th. f. Heb. *hallel* 'praise' + *Jah* >Jehovah, the Lord.

Halloween

C18th. f. OE. *halig* 'holy' and *oefen* 'evening'. In the old Celtic calendar, this was the night of all the witches. As so often, the church transformed it into a Christian festival, the eve of All Saints, which follows.

Ham

OE., meaning 'bend of the knee'; C17th., thigh of a hog; a Germanic word. The root means 'be crooked'.

Hamburger

C20th. Nothing to do with the above. The meat is beef, and the derivation is from the city of Hamburg, much as frankfurters are from Frankfurt.

Hammock

C16th. f. Sp. *hamaca*, of Caribbean origin. One of those words brought to Europe by travellers.

Hand

OE. A widespread Germanic word – Ger. and Du. have it – that doesn't exist anywhere else.

Hara-kiri

C19th. Japanese *hara* 'belly' and *kiri* 'cut'. The novelist Yakuo Mishima committed it in 1970.

Hare

OE. f. a Germanic root meaning 'grey'.

Harem

C17th. f. Arab. *haram* 'place for women only'.

Harlot

C16th. The word is sometimes traced back to Arlette, the unmarried mother of William the Conquerer, but this is (probably) a slur on her reputation. Before C16th. the word was applied to men, and this is how Chaucer, for example, uses it, to mean 'vagabond'. It comes f. OFr.

herlot. Collins compares this to the degeneration of the word 'tramp' to mean 'prostitute'.

Harm
OE. f. Pers. *sarm.*

Harp
OE. a Germanic word. Du. has it.

Harpsichord
C17th. This is 'harp' + 'chord' ('string'). Where the 's' has crept in from is not known. It. is *arpicordo.*

Hartebeest
C18th. f. Afrikaans *hartbees.*

Harvest
OE. This word has an IE. root which can be seen in Gk. *karpos* 'fruit'. It comes to Eng. through the Germanic languages. OHG. is *herbest.*

Hashish
C16th. f. Arab. *hasis* 'herb'.

Hat
OE. a Germanic word (Du. has it) with an IE. root meaning 'covering'.

Hate
OE. a Germanic word: OHG. is *hazzon*, ModGer. *hut.* There is an IE. root. which produced, among other words Irish *caiss* 'strong feeling'.

Haversack
C18th. f. Ger. *Haber* 'oats' + *sack.* It was where the cavalry carried oats for their horses.

Havoc
C15th. f. ON. *havoc*, of unknown origin.

Hawk
OE. a Germanic word. ModGer. is *Habicht.*

Hay
OE. a Germanic word. ModGer. is *Heu.*

Hazel
OE. a Germanic word. ModGer. is *Hasel.* There is an IE. root which also led to L. *corylus.*

Head
OE. a Germanic word with an IE. root which also led to L. *caput*, f. which Eng. gets 'captain' and many other words.

Heart
OE. This word and other words to do with the heart ('cardiac' etc.) go back to the same root. The IE. base led to OE. *heorte* as well as words in most European languages: Gk. is *kardia*, L. *cord*, Dutch *hart*.

Heathen
OE. orig. someone who lived on the heath, which is also OE. The word came to mean a 'non-Christian' under the influence of L. *paganus* >pagan, C14th., 'country dweller'.

Heaven
OE. unc. orig., but the OE. *heofon* has correspondences in most northern European languages, for example, Ger. *Himmel*.

Hebrew
C13th. orig. an Aramaic word meaning 'one from the other side of the river', it went into Gk. *Hebraios* and then into L.

Hedonist
C19th. f. Gk. *hedone* 'pleasure'. *Hedys* = 'sweet'.

Helicopter
C19th. f. Gk. *helios* 'spiral' and *pteron* 'wing'. The word was coined to denote the first unsuccessful attempts to do what the C20th. planes can do.

Hell
OE. a Germanic word. OHG. is *hella*.

Help
OE. a Germanic word. OHG. is *helfan*.

Hemi-
This Gk. prefix means the same as >semi. So 'hemisphere', C14th. (*sphaira* 'globe').

Hen
OE. a Germanic word. OHG. is *henna*.

Hermaphrodite
C15th. in Gk. mythology, the son of <u>Hermes</u> and <u>Aphrodite</u>, who had both male and female sexual characteristics.

Hero
C14th. f. Gk. *heros* through L. The Ger. word *Heroin*, C19th., was said to have been invented because of delusions of strength suffered by addicts, but this seems fanciful.

Hetero
This Gk. prefix denotes 'other'. So 'heterosexual', prob. C20th.

Heyday
C16th. f. L. *heidi* 'hurrah!', which has no connection with the girls' given name, which is a Swiss version of a Ger. word meaning 'nobility'.

Hiccup
C16th. imit. The word is sometimes written as 'hiccough', which is either a genteelism, or a confusion through association with 'cough'.

Hide
OE. a Germanic word. MD. is *hydan*.

Higgledy-piggledy
C16th. prob. based on >pig; it suggests brilliantly a load of the creatures at the sow's teats or the trough.

High
OE. a Germanic word. OHG. is *hoh*.

Hippodrome
C16th. f. Gk. *hippo* horse + *drome* race. C19th., used for 'music hall'. >aerodrome, >dromedary, >palindrome, >syndrome for unlikely connections.

Hippopotamus
C16th. f. Gk. *hippo* 'horse' + *potamos* 'river'.

History
C15th. f. Gk. *histor* 'learned man'.

Hoax
>hocus-pocus

Hockey
C19th. of unknown origin, but possibly related to a word for 'crooked'.

Hocus-pocus
C17th. Both *Chambers* and Hitchings suggest that this comes f. a satirical, probably Puritanical (Hitchings), version of that part of the Catholic Mass *Hoc est corpus meum* 'This is my body'. Hoad quotes *hax pax max meus Deus adimax*, a cod-L. formula chorused by students, probably after a few bevvies. So conjurers used it. 'Hoax', C18th. is derived from it.

Hogmanay
C17th. Sc. the last day of the year. The Normans brought *hoguinane* or *aguillanneuf* a 'new year's gift'. So write Hoad and Ayto. *SOED* agrees. But Hitchings mentions other possibilities: a Celt. version of Gk. *hagia mene* 'holy month', a corruption of L. *hoc anno novo*, where 'new year' is visible, and 'a rendering of the druids' cry *Au gui l'an neuf*'. A less likely

suggestion is that it is a corruption of 'Hug me Now'. And Webster says, simply, origin unknown.

Hoi polloi
C19th. means 'the ordinary people': Gk. 'the people'; note: to say '*the* hoi polloi' is to say 'the' twice.

Holiday
OE. *haligdaeg*, 'holy' + 'day'.

Holocaust
C13th. f. Gk. *holos* 'whole' and *kaustos*, a form of the verb 'burn'.

Holy
OE. *halig*. The root is a Germanic one meaning 'whole', and means something pure and unviolated.

Home
OE. a Germanic word of obscure origin. OHG. is *heim*.

Homeopathy
C20th. f. Gk. *homo* 'same' + *pathy* 'suffering, feeling'; so, the attempted treatment of a disease with infinitesimal doses of the disease.

Homosexual
1897. Note that *homo*- is nothing to do with L. *homo* 'man', but f. Gk. *homo* 'same'. >gay, >sex.

Honey
OE. The IE. root is present in Eng. 'mellifluous' and in the name *Melissa* (Gk. 'honeybee). The word for the stuff itself, though, is Germanic: Ger. itself has *Honig*.

Honest
C13th. f. L. *honestus*. When Hamlet asks Ophelia 'are you honest?' (3:1) he is asking her, insultingly, if she is chaste, an earlier meaning of the word, along with 'decent'.

Hooch
C20th. f. the name of the N. American tribe *Hoochinoo*, members of which are supposed to have made poor quality and illicit alcohol.

Hooligan
C19th. 'The name of an Irish family in south-east London conspicuous for its ruffianism' (*SOED*). *Chambers* points out that this could have come f. a music hall song.

Horizon
C14th. f. Gk. *horos* 'boundary'.

Horizontal
C16th. 'to do with the >horizon'.

Horrible
C14th. f. L. *horrere* '[hair] stand on end'. 'Horrid', C16th., harks back to this meaning: 'bristling'.

Hors d'oeuvre
C18th. to mean 'starter'. *Hors* is 'outside' and *oevre* 'work'. A starter is, etymologically, not part of the meal. To be *hors de combat* is to be 'out of the battle', probably through injury.

Horse
OE. *hors*. The L. *equus* died out in favour of the Germanic word, but survives in 'equestrian' and 'equine'.

Hosanna
f. Heb. *hosah-na* 'save, pray'; through Gk. and L.

Hospice
>hospital.

Hospital
C13th. 'a place to say' (think of 'hospitality' and 'hospice'); eventually, C16th., 'place for the care of the sick'. f. OF. *hospital*, which survives in Modern Fr. *hopital*, and MedL. *hospitale*.

Hot
OE. a Germanic word. Ger. is *Heiss*.

Hotchpotch
C15th. Improbable as it sounds, this is f. OFr. *hocher* 'shake' and *pot*.

House
OE. *hus*. a Germanic word. Ger. is *Haus*; beyond that, of obscure origin.

Hubris
C19th. Gk. 'insolence'.

Hug
C16th. of unknown origin. But *Chambers* points out that OIce. *hugga* is 'comfort'.

Human
C14th. f. L. *humanus*, related to *homo* 'man'.

Hurricane
C16th. f. Sp. *huracan*, Port. *furacao*; of Caribbean origin, brought back by Iberian explorers. >hammock.

Husband
OE. f. ON. *hus* 'house' + *bondi* 'dwell'.

Hussy
C16th. a reduction of *huswif* 'housewife'.

Hydr(o)-
Prefix denoting 'water', as in 'hydrophobia', C16th., 'fear of water'.
>phobia.

Hygiene
C19th. f. Gk. *hugies* 'healthy'. There is an IE. root meaning 'well-living'.

Hyper-
This prefix denotes 'over', 'above' etc. f. Gk. *huper*; so 'hyperbole', C16th,
(Gk. *ballein* 'to throw'). Hyperactive is an obvious C20th. example.

Hysteria
C19th. was thought be a result of uterine problems; modern L., f. Gk.
hustera 'womb'.

I

I
OE. *ic.* Versions of the first person pronoun, unsurprisingly, are everywhere in the languages descending f. the IE. root: Gk. and L. >*ego*, Sanskr. *aham*, Hittite *uk*, modern Fr. *Je*, ModGer. *ich*, modern Du. *ik*.

Ice
OE. a Germanic word, not traceable back further. ON. is *iss*. 'Iceberg', C18th., is f. a Danish word for 'ice mountain'.

Icon
C16th. 'image'. f. Gk. *eikon* 'likeness'. C20th., the word has dropped to mean a 'public figure'. 'Iconoclast', C17th. (*eikon* + *klan* 'break') became current to describe puritan extremists who smashed images of saints etc. in churches.

Idea
C16th. Gk. *idein* 'see'. Plato developed the idea of the 'nature of something'. 'Ideology', C18th., is 'the science of ideas' (>logy).

Idiot
C13th. f. Gk. *idiotes* 'private person'; then it took on the sense of 'layman', someone ignorant. It came to Eng. through L. *idiota* with its present meaning.

Idle
OE., C13th. 'lazy'; a Germanic word. Ger. has *eitel* 'vain': the primary meaning is 'empty'; of unknown origin.

Idol
C13th. f. Gk. *eidolon*, which is related to >idea, through L.

Igloo
C14th. f. Inuktitut.

Ignorant
C13th. f. L. *ignorare* 'not knowing'.

Iguana
C16th. Sp., of Caribbean origin.

Ill
C13th. ON. *illr.*, and meaning 'bad' (as in 'ill-will'). Origin beyond that is unknown.

Illustrate
C16th. f. L. *in-* + *lustrare* 'make bright'.

Im-
>in-

Immaculate
C15th. L. *macula* = 'stain' and the first syllable of this word is a negative. The only examples of 'maculate' that I have come across are in Shakespeare's *Love's Labour's Lost* 1:2, to mean 'stained, polluted', and in poems by T S Eliot, Elizabeth Bishop and Geoffrey Hill. Bishop talks of a 'maculate, cherished' house.

Image
C13th. f. L. *imago*. 'Imagine', C14th. f. *imaginare* 'form an image of'.

Imam
C17th. Arab. 'leader'.

Imperial
>emperor

Im-, In-
These L. prefixes have two possible meanings. One is 'in', 'into' 'within' etc. Some examples, im- first: 'imperil', C16th. (*periculum* 'risk'); 'implicate', C16th. (*plicare* 'fold'); 'import', C15th. (*portare* 'bring'); *in-*: 'incandescent', C18th. (*candescere* 'become white'); 'incarcerate', C17th. (*carcer* 'prison'); 'increase', C14th. (*crescere* 'grow'). There are many others.

The other is a negative, >ignorant. Some examples are: (im- first) 'immense', C15th. (*metiri* 'measure': the word means, literally 'unmeasurable'); 'immortal', C14th. (*mortalis*); 'impatience', C13th. (*patientia* 'suffering'); *in-*: 'incessant', C16th. (*cessare* 'cease'); incest, C13th. (*castus* 'chase'); 'insincere' (>sincere). There are many others.

The prefix is changed to *il-* before 'l', for example, 'illegal', C17th., and 'illiterate', C16th.

Inch
OE. f. L. *uncial* 'twelfth'. In these decimal days, it is still used as a verb.

Index
C16th. L. 'forefinger'.

Indigo
C16th. The plant which the blue dye comes from is *Indigofera*. f. Gk. *indikon* 'indian dye'.

Inept
C16th. f. L. negative >*in-*, *aptus* = 'fitting'.

Infant
C14th. f. L. negative >*in-* + *fari* 'speak'.

Influenza
C18th. It. for 'influence', and so 'outbreak' as in *influenza di catarro* 'outbreak of catarrh'. The abbreviation 'flu' is C19th.

Infra-
This L. prefix. means 'under', 'below', etc.; so 'infra-red' (C19th.) rays are rays that lie beyond the red end of the spectrum; 'infra-dig' (C19th) is an abbreviation of L. *infra dignitatem* 'beneath one's dignity'.

Ink
C13th. f. Gk. *egkauston* 'purple ink'.

Inn
OE. A Germanic root. An inn is simply somewhere where you are 'in'.

Inter-
This L. prefix means 'between', 'among'. So 'intercede', C16th., (*cedere* 'go'); interfere', C16th. (*ferire* 'strike'); 'interrupt', C15th. (*rumpere* 'break'). But . . .

Inter
C14th. . . . this verb is not one of the inter- words. f. L. *in-* + *terra* 'earth'.

Interim
C16th. L. Hoad says it is 'archaic', but I still hear it, a slightly pompous synonym for 'meantime'.

Iron
OE. prob. f. Celt. *isarno*, though it has cousins in Germanic languages: *Eisen* in German, for example.

Irony
C16th. no connection with >iron. f. Ger. *Eironeia* 'feigned ignorance'; now, 'saying the opposite of what is meant'. It is currently coming to mean 'coincidental' as in 'Ironically, it was on the same ground that Smith scored his last hattrick'. Much as change is inevitable, this one is regrettable.

Islam
C19th. Arab. 'Surrender to God'.

Island

OE. *Egland*, later *iland*. The Germanic root *aujo* is not specifically to do with islands, but means 'land associated with water'. The related L. *aqua* gives Eng. 'aquarium', C19th., etc. The 's' wasn't acquired till C16th., by a confusion with the next (etymologically unrelated) word.

Isle

C12th. f. L. *insula*, the origin of which is obscure. Eng. gets 'insular', C17th., and 'peninsula', C16th., from it.

Itch

OE. common in Germanic languages, as no doubt the thing was in life. OHG. has *jucchem* and is visible in ModGer. *Juckreiz*.

Ivory

C13th. f. L. *ebor*, through Fr. *ivurie*. It may have come from an Egyptian word.

Ivy

OE. a Germanic word of unc. orig.

J

Jack
C14th. *jakke* 'mechanical device'. The word was developed f. the given name, which has been used for machines, male workers and male animals. 'Jackdaw' is C16th.; 'Jack-Tar' is C17th.; 'Jack-knife' is C18th., as is 'jackass'. 'Jack-of-all-trades' and 'steeplejack' are C19th.

Jackal
C17th., is etymologically unconnected with the above. f. Pers. *sakal*.

Jacuzzi
C20th. a trademark word for that swirly bath.

Jail
>gaol

Jalopy
C20th. US. of unknown origin.

Jambalaya
C19th. US. Louisiana Fr., f. Provencale *jambalaia*.

Jam
C18th. 'to get stuck together', now usually in traffic; of unknown origin, as is the name of the sweet stuff in a jar; though the sweet stuff is fruit 'jammed' together.

Jargon
C14th. to mean 'twittering of birds', then 'meaningless words'; C17th. 'debased language'; then speech for a particular profession; now often derogatory; though what trade, from architecture to zoology, from bee-keeping to yoga, could do without its jargon? f. OF. *jargoun*.

Jasmine
C16th. ult. a Pers. word *yasmin* which has come to us through Arab. and Fr.

Javelin
C16th. f. Celt. through OFr. OIr. is *gabul*.

Jaw
C14th. f. OFr. *joe*. of unc. orig.

Jazz
C20th. of unknown origin. There are, apparently, many possible African words which may have bequeathed an earlier word. One is *jasm* 'energy'. The word is often said to mean 'sexual intercourse'.

Jehovah
C16th. meaning The LORD, the word arose something like this: Hebrew was not vocalized, and given as YHWH. This was considered too holy to pronounce, so the vowels of *donay* 'my Lord' were inserted. The combination produced 'Jehovah'. >Hallelujah.

Jeep
C12th. A trademark name. >Jacuzzi.

Jerusalem artichoke
C17th. The first word is a corruption of It. *girasole* 'sunflower'. The Jerusalem artichoke is neither from Jerusalem nor an artichoke.

Jesus
C12th. This word, the L. version, comes f. Aramaic, the language Jesus spoke. This word was not used in OE., where it was rendered as *Haelend*, Saviour. f. Hebrew/Aramaic *Yhosua*, our 'Joshua', 'Yahveh is salvation'.

Jew
C12th. f. the patriarchal name *Judah*. (Gen. 29.35). It comes to us through L. *judaeus*.

Jew's harp
C16th. is nothing to do with the above. The thing is played by plucking metal strings that are pulled across a tiny iron frame. You do this close to the mouth. Notes are achieved by various shaping of the mouth. Possibly f. 'jaw's harp'.

Jezebel
C16th. meaning 'shameless woman', it derives f. the infamous wife of Ahab in the Old Testatement 1 Kgs 16.31.

Jig
C16th. of unknown origin, though possibly f. middle Fr. *gigeur*.

Jiggery-pokery
C19th. 'Cheating behaviour', this word may come f. Sc. dialect *jookery-pawkery*.

Jihad
C19th. Arab. 'struggle'.

Jingoism
C19th. 'excessive patriotism'. f. a music hall song 'We don't want to fight but by jingo if we do . . .', the substance of the rest of which can be imagined.

Jinx
C20th. f. Gk *inyx* through L., a bird (the wryneck) used in spells.

Job
C16th. origin unknown.

Jockey
C16th. the pet form of Jock.

Jockstrap
C20th. Since C18th., the first part of the word has been slang for >penis.

Jodhpur
C19th. f. the name of a town in N. W. India.

Joke
C17th. orig. slang, possibly comes f. L. *jocus* 'jest', which came into OFr. as *jeu*.

Jolly
C14th. Perhaps f. the name of an ON. midwinter festival *jol*; and perhaps, on the other hand, f. OFr. *jolif*.

Journal
C14th. 'service book'; by C18th., 'daily newspaper'. f. L. *diurnalis* 'occupying a day'.

Journey
C13th. 'day's travel'. f. L. *diurnam* 'daily portion' through Fr.

Jovial
C16th. f. the name of the Roman god *Jove*, through It. *giovale*. The second two syllables of *Jupiter* (another name for Jove) are related to L. *pater*. >father.

Joy
C13th. f. L. *gaudere* 'rejoice', through Fr. *joye*, f. which we get 'enjoy' and 'rejoice'.

Jubilee
C14th., 'fiftieth anniversary'. f. Heb. *yobhel* 'ram's horn', which was blown to announce the special year that the Hebrews kept every fifty (Lev. 25). 'Jubilation', C14th., and 'jubilant', C17th., are f. L. *jubilare*, and are not etymologically connected.

Juggernaut
C17th. f. Sanskr. *Jagannatha* 'world' + 'protector', Krishna's title, and thence the large carriage on which his idol was carried.

Jujitsu
C19th. f. Japanese *ju* 'gentle' and *jutsu* 'science'.

Jump
C16th. of unknown origin, perhaps imit? The soft 'j' the take-off, the 'mp' the sound of landing? Like 'bump', 'thump'.

Jungle
C18th. f. Sanskr. *jangala* 'arid region'.

Juvenile
C17th. f. L. *juvenis* 'young'.

K

Kaleidoscope
C19th. f. Gk. *kalos* 'beautiful' + *eidos* 'shape' + *scope* 'observational instrument'.

Kamasutra
C19th. f. Sanskr. *kama* 'love' + *sutra* 'thread', 'rule'.

Kamikazi
C20th. Japanese *kami* 'divine' + *kazi* 'wind'. Hitchings writes that 'a wind . . . destroyed a fleet of invading Mongols in 1281'.

Kangaroo
C18th. f. Native Australian, spoken in Queensland, *kangooroo*, according to the explorer James Cook (1770).

Kaput
C19th. f. Ger. *kaputt* 'broken'. Fr. *faire capot* is to beat at cards by taking all the tricks; of unc. orig.

Karaoke
C20th. Japanese *kara* 'empty' + *oke*, 'orchestra'.

Karate
C20th. Japanese *kara* 'empty' + *te* 'hand'.

Karma
C19th. Sanskr. 'action, effect, fate'. It means 'destiny as decided by actions in a previous life'.

Kayak
C18th. f. Inuktitut *kajakka* 'boat made of skins', through Danish.

Kebab
C17th. f. Arab. *kabab* 'roasted meat', through Pers.

Keep
OE. of unknown origin for both the verb and for the noun, C13th., meaning 'central building of a castle'.

Kerfuffle
C20th. f. Scand. *carfuffle* then Sc. *curfuffle*.

Kestrel
C15th. f. L. *crepitaculum* 'rattle', through Fr. *crecerelle*. Perhaps of imit. origin.

Ketchup
C18th. f. Chinese *koetsiap*, 'brine of pickled fish', through Malay.

Kettle
C13th. a Germanic word – Ger. is *Kessel* – with a L. root *catinus*; in another form *catillus* 'vessel used for cooking and serving food'.

Key
OE. f. OFriesian *kei*, but otherwise of unknown origin, and with no relatives in other Germanic languages. There is a close relationship between Frisian and Eng.

Khaki
C19th. Urdu, f. Pers. 'dusty'. One of the words from the British Raj in India.

Kibbutz
C20th. modern Heb. *qibbus*, 'gathering'.

Kibosh
C19th. Origin unknown, but perhaps f. 'bosh'.

Kick
C14th. a word with no relatives in other IE. languages. Fr. has no word. You have to say *donner un coup de pied*, 'to give a hit with the foot'.

Kid
C12th. 'Young goat'; C16th., 'child'. A Germanic word with no cognates elsewhere. So 'kidnapper', C17th., US.: 'napper' is a cant word for 'thief'. The 'kids' were 'napped' to supply slaves for plantations.

Kill
C13th. 'strike', a century later for modern meaning; a Germanic word of obscure origin.

Kilo-
This prefix is f. Gk. *khilioi* and usually denotes one thousand, as in 'kilometre', 'a thousand metres', though a 'kilobyte' is 1024 bytes.

Kin
OE. 'family'; a Germanic word with an IE. root that produced L. *genus* and Gk. *gene* among others. Swedish *kox* 'sex' is another product of the Germanic branch.

Kine-

These words comes f. Gk. *kinein* 'move'. C20th. Thus, 'kinematic' describes sculpture that moves, and the 'kinema' (original spelling) shows us moving pictures.

Kind

OE. f. a Germanic word which passed into OE. as *gecynde*, the first part of which was lost in the Middle Ages.

King

OE. A Germanic word related to Du. *koning* and Ger. *Konig*.

Kiosk

C19th. Words have a way of losing dignity (>slogan, >iconic, >charisma), and this word comes f. the Pers. *kusk* 'palace'. Fr. is *kiosque* 'bandstand', which seems to bridge the dignified with the commonplace.

Kirk

C12th. northern and Sc. 'church' f. ON. *kirkja*.

Kiss

OE. A widespread Germanic word. Ger. has *Kussen*, Sw. *kyssa*. It is probably imit., and goes back to an IE. root.

Kitchen

OE. f. late L. *coquina*, f. *coquere* 'cook'. Versions of it spread throughout the empire: Fr. *cuisine*, while West Ger. had *Kocina*; whence Du. *keuken* and our word.

Kleptomania

>mania

Knack

C16th. 'dexterity with a tool' etc. but it also meant, C14th., 'sharp hit', so the word is probably imit. Both Du. and LG. have *knak*.

Knee

OE. A brotherhood word going back to an IE. root. It is visibly there in Hittite, Sanskr., Gk, L., and OIr. respectively: *kenu, janu, gonu, genu, glun*. Fr. has *genou*, Ger. *Knie*, It. *ginocchio*. We can see the word's origins clearly in 'genuflect', 'to bend the knee in worship'.

Knickers

C19th. Diedrich Knickerbocker was the pretended author of Washington Irvine's *History of New York* (1809). The garment got its name from the illustrations by George Cruikshank.

Knife

C11th. f. Old Norse *kniffr*. You can see it in modern Fr. *canif*, but its origins are obscure.

Knot
OE. a Germanic word. Ger. for example, is *Knoten*.

Know
C11th. f. an IE. base from which L. gets *noscere* (and f. which Eng. gets 'cognisant'). Other words in the family have OIc. *gnath*, for example, and Sanskr. *janati*.

Knuckle
C14th. a Germamic word. Ger. has *Knochel*.

Kodak
C19th. A trademark word, invented randomly by George Eastman in 1888.

Koran
>qur'an

Kosher
C19th. f. Heb. *hasher* 'right'.

L

Labour
C13th. f. L. *labor* 'trouble, exertion', maybe related to *labere* 'slip'.

Labyrinth
C16th. f. Gk. *laburinthos*, a word f. a pre-Gk. culture.

Lackadaisical
C18th. an extended form of 'lack-a-day'. Perhaps the change in meaning came about because of the similar >lax.

Laconic
C16th. The *Lakons* from Sparta in Ancient Greece were famous for their not saying much. An enemy general besieging their city told them that if they did not surrender, everything in the city would be put to flames. The Lakons replied, 'If'.

Lad
C13th. 'Servant man'; C16th. 'youth'; ME *ladde*, origin unknown.

Lady
OE. *hlaf* = bread and -*dig* = 'knead' are just visible presences in this word. A lady was a bread-maker. >loaf. This word exists only in Eng. *Hlaf* led to 'dough' and -*dig* to *dough*. 'Lord', also OE., is the 'keeper of the loaf'.

Ladybird
C16th. The lady named here is possibly Mary, Jesus' mother, though the Nurse calls Juliet 'ladybird' to mean something like >sweetheart (*Romeo and Juliet* 1:3).

Lager
C19th. f. Ger. *Lager* 'store'.

Lake
C13th. f. L. *lacus* 'basin', f. *lacuna* 'hole'. 'Lacuna', C17th., is a 'gap in a manuscript'. The original sense was 'hole'; water came secondarily. Irish and Sc. *loch* are related, and so is 'lagoon', C17th.

Lallans
C18th. a Sc. origin, or variant, of 'Lowlands'.

Lama
C17th. This Buddhist priest takes the name f. Tibetan *blama* (the 'b' is silent).

Lamb
OE. a Germanic word (Ger. and Swed. have *lamm*). No cousins are known outside this group.

Lamp
C12th. f. Gk. *lampas* 'torch'.

Land
OE. a Germanic word, and although there is an IE. base, it is only visible in Germanic languages; but it's there in Cornish and Welsh placenames like *Llangollen*, where it denotes 'empty space' and later 'church'.

Language
C13th. ult. f. L. *lingua* 'tongue', through OFr. *langage*.

Lark
OE. *lawerce*, related to many various words in Germanic languages: MD. is *lerche*. There is a Sc. version *laverock* that descends f. ME. *laverok*.

Lascivious
C15th. f. L. *lascivia*.

Laser
C20th. An acronym: **L**ight **A**mplification by **S**timulated **E**mission of **R**adiation.

Lass
C13th. *lasce*, of obscure origin There is a possibility that it may be related to an Old Swed. word for 'unmarried'.

Late
OE. a Germanic word with an IE. root that also passed into L. *lassus* 'weary', which Eng. has in 'alas', C13th., and 'lassitude', C16th.

Laugh
OE. *hlaehhan*. Versions are everywhere in Germanic languages: Ger. and Du. are *lachen*. f. the IE. root. Gk. gets *klossein* 'cluck'. So presumably the word is of imit. origin.

Lavatory
C14th. An IE. root produced, among other words, L. *lavare* 'wash' and then 'lavabo', a place dedicated to the ritual washing of the Christian

priest's hands before Mass. Its current usage to mean 'room with a water closet', C18th., is a euphemism.

Lax
f. L. *laxus* 'loose-bowelled', f. which Eng. gets 'laxative', C14th.

Lazy
C16th. This word replaced 'slack' and is of obscure origin.

Learn
OE. f. a Germanic word. OHG. is *lernen*.

Lecher
C12th. f. Frankish *likken*, f. a Germanic root meaning 'lick'.

Left
C13th. This word is of unknown origin. It is there is some Germanic languages, and has pejorative implications, meaning 'weak' or 'worthless'. Note that the left side of a church, the north side as you face the altar (and the morning sun), is also less respected than the other sides.

Leg
C13th. The OE. word is *shank*, which we have in the expression, 'to use shank's pony', that is, to walk, and the dish 'lamb's shank'. 'Leg' is f. ON. *leggr*. Only Swed. and Danish have the word among Germanic languages, and then only for 'calf'. According to the English traveller and writer Frederick Marryat (*Diary in America*, 1837, quoted by Bryson) the word was considered indecent in the US. in polite society. He asked a young woman if she had hurt her leg in a fall, and she blushed and told him that people did not use that word in America. Apparently, he should have used 'limb'. In some contexts, it is still common to use 'dark meat' for 'thigh' when eating chicken, and 'white meat' when eating >breast.

Lemon
C14th. f. Pers. *limun* through Arab.

Lens
C17th. f. L. *lens* 'lentil', so-called because of the shape. Lentil, C13th. is f. L. *lenticula*, a diminutive of *lens*.

Leopard
C13th. f. Gk. *leopardus* through L. The first part meant 'lion', the second 'panther'.

Leprechaun
C17th. Irish, of course. *Lu* = 'small'. But the last part of the word is f. L. *corpus* 'body'.

Lesbian
C19th. f. the name of the Gk. island Lesbos where the poet Sappho
(*c*.600 BC), reputedly a homosexual, lived. This depends on a simplistic
reading of her (few) extant lines of poetry.

Lettuce
C13th. f. L. *lac* 'milk'. There's a milky white sap when the stalk is cut,
apparently.

Lewd
OE. This word orig. meant 'lay, not clerical' and is of unknown origin.

Lexicographer
C17th. A dictionary compiler or, as the great one, Dr Johnson put it, 'a
harmless drudge'. Its roots are in the Gk. *lexicon* 'wordbook' and *graphein*
'write' >graph.

Liaison
C17th. meaning 'thickening of sauces', and by C19th 'illicit relation-
ship'; f. L. *ligare* 'bind', f. which Fr. gets *lier*. 'Liaise' is a back formation.
(See p 207).

Libido
C20th. L. 'sexual desire' or 'instinct'. >ego, >superego.

Library
C14th. f. L. *libraria* 'bookshop', which is the meaning of Fr. *librarie*.

Lie
OE. 'be prostrate'; a Germanic word (OHG. is *liggen*) with an IE. root
which also appears in Gk. *lektron* and L. *lectus*, both 'bed'. It is unconnected to the word meaning 'untruth', also OE. and also Germanic
(Ger. has *Lugen*).

Life
OE. A Germanic word. Ger. has *Leben* 'live'.

Light
OE. There are two distinct words. The one for 'illumination' is
Germanic (Ger. has *Licht*) f. an IE. root that also led to Gk. *leukos* 'white'
and L. *lux*. The word for 'of little weight' is also Germanic (Ger. has
Leicht 'easy') with an IE. root.

Limbo
C13th. a place for things or people forgotten; then (according to
Roman Catholic teaching, now abandoned) a place for souls who had
lived before the resurrection of Christ, and unbaptized infants. f. L.
limbus 'hem'.

Limerick
C19th. possibly f. the phrase 'Will you come up to Limerick?' sung in between limericks, but there seems to be no evidence for this. Oddly the word wasn't used until after Edward Lear's death, who composed many (to our ears) tame examples.

Limey
C20th. Aust., Canadian and US. slang for Br. person, especially a sailor. A folk etymology says that it comes from the expression 'Cor blimey!', but in fact it's a contraction of 'lime-juicer': lime was given to Br. sailors to counteract scurvy.

Lingerie
C19th. f. L. *lineus* 'linen' through Fr. *linge*.

Lion
ME. f. Gk. *leon*.

Liquid
C14th. f. L. *liquere* 'be fluid'.

Little
OE. a Germanic word. OHG. is *luzzil* and Du. *luttel*.

Lizard
C14th. f. L. *lacerta*, of unc. orig., which also meant 'muscle'; presumably from a perceived resemblance.

Loaf
OE. *hlaf*. >lord, >lady.

Lobster
OE. f. L. *locusta*, which also meant 'locust', C13th., both for the marauding insect, and for the fruit of the carob, which was, according to Hoad, eaten by John the Baptist (Mt. 3.4); though most authorities insist he was eating the insect.

Logic
C14th. f. L. *logica*, but ult. f. Gk. *logika*.

-logy
This Gk. prefix denotes 'study'. Thus >etymology, and >neurology, and many others.

Long
A Germanic word (Ger., Du., Swed. *lang*). It is related to L. *longus*, but it has not been shown how.

Lord
>lady

Lorry
C19th. of unknown origin.

Lounge
C16th. of unknown origin.

Love
OE. Unsurprisingly 'the word known to all men' (to quote a central idea in *Ulysses* by James Joyce) has an IE. root that leads to Ger. *Liebe* and L. *libido* 'strong desire', and many other words in many other languages. Ger. *Lob* and Du. *lof* (both 'praise') are related.

Luck
C15th. a Germanic word (Ger. *Gluck*) of unknown origin.

Ludo
C20th. This dice-and-board children's game is an example of how modern things, even the most banal, have classical names because their inventors or publishers have been educated at public school. f. L. *ludere* 'play'. 'Ludicrous', C17th., is f. the same word.

Lullaby
C16th. This word is imit., f. soothing sounds made to help a baby to sleep. *Chambers* dates its first use 1588. Shakespeare's use of it in *A Midsummer Night's Dream* (2:3), *c*.1594–1596 shows how up-to-date he could be with new words (not counting the ones he invented. >puke).

Lunatic
C13th. f. L. *luna* 'moon'. The moon's been blamed for madness, love and poetry: 'the lunatic, the lover and poet' are bunched together by Theseus in *A Midsummer Night's Dream* 5:1. The IE. base also produced 'light'. >moon.

Lunch
C16th. f. Sp., possibly, *lonja* 'slice'; successively 'hunk of bread' and 'snack'. The modern meaning arrived in C19th.

Lust
OE. a Germanic word. Ger. *Lust* is 'pleasure'.

Luxury
C14th. f. L. *luxuria* 'excess'.

Lychee
C16th. f. Chinese *li-tchi*.

Lycra
C20th. A trademark.

Lynch
C19th. Captain William Lynch of Virginia set up tribunals to try suspects, with appalling consequences, the 'strange fruit hanging from the poplar trees' in Lewis Allan's great song, often performed by Billie Holiday.

Lyric
C13th. f. Gk. *lura* 'lyre'.

M

Macabre
C15th. f. Fr. *Dance Macabre* 'dance of death'; OFr. was *Macabe* (Eng. Maccabees) and the word refers to a play about the slaughter of Jewish group with this name. The story is told in the Aprocrypha.

Macaroni
C16th. It. f. Gk. *makaria* 'food made from barley'. C18th., the word meant 'foppish man', probably because such men enjoyed, or maybe affected to enjoy, foreign food. It is Aust. rhyming slang for >baloney. 'Macaroon', C17th, is ult. f. the same word, but through Fr.

Machiavellian
C15th. Niccolo Machiavelli was a Florentine statesman (1469–1527) who argued in his book *Il Principe* (*The Prince)* that rulers should place advantage over morality. No change there, then.

Macaw
C17th. f. Port. *macao*, of unknown origin.

Machine
C16th. f. Gk. *machos* 'contrivance'. L. *mechanicus* led to 'mechanical'.

Macho and machismo
>male.

Macro-
This prefix denotes 'large'. 'Macroeconomics', C20th., denotes the 'economics of the world'. >micro.

Mad
C13th. This word has an IE. root which passed into OE. as *gemad*. The first syllable disappeared. L. *mutare*, f. the same root, suggests that the original meaning was 'change'. The underlying idea is that a mad person is a changed person.

Madam
C13th. f. OFr. *ma* + *dame* 'my lady'. 'Madonna' goes back to the same root: It. *mia* + *donna* 'lady'.

Maelstrom
Du. *maelstrom* (now *malstroom)*; f. *maalen* 'grind' + *stroom* 'stream'.

Maestro
>master.

Mafia
C19th. f. a Sicilian dialect meaning 'hostility to the law' or 'boldness'.
The word may go back to Arab. *mahjas* 'boldness, aggression'.

Magazine
C16th. f. Arab. *kazana* 'store up' and then *makazin*. A modern magazine
may store armaments, C16th., information, C17th., or articles, C18th.

Magnolia
C17th. f. the name of the botanist Pierre Magnol (1638–1715).

Maharajah
C17th. f. Hindi, ult. f. Sanskr. *maha* 'great' + *rajah* 'king'.

Mahatma
C19th. f. Sanskr. *maha* 'great' + *atman* 'soul'.

Maiden
OE. a Germanic word, widespread in northern Europe – ModGer.
is *Madchen* – that goes back to an IE. root which produced Irish *mug*
'slave'.

Mah-jong
C20th. Shanghai dialect Chinese for 'house sparrow'; named after a
design of the pieces used in this game.

Major-
C16th. L. 'greater', stemming f. *magnus* 'large', f. whence Eng. 'magni-
tude', C14th.

Mal-
This L. prefix often denotes 'evil' or 'badness'. So, a few examples: 'mal-
efactor', C15th. (*facere* 'do'); 'malevolent', C16th., (*velle* 'will'); malice is
C13th.; 'malfunction' is C20th.

Malapropism
C19th. In Sheridan's play *The Rivals* (1775) Mrs Malaprop, always trying
to sound grand, constantly misuses words: 'as headstrong as an allegory
on the banks of the Nile'. Dogberry does something similar, though
without the grandiloquent motives, in Shakespeare's *Much Ado About
Nothing*: 'Oh villain! Thou wilt be condemned into everlasting redemp-
tion for this.' Sheridan invented the name with care: it was borrowed
(C17th.) f. Fr. *mal a propos* 'bad for the purpose'.

Malaria
C18th. f. It. *mala* 'bad' + *aria* 'air'. The illness was once thought to come from marshy places.

Malarkey
C20th. meaning 'nonsense', this word is of unknown origin. Hitchings notes that *malaka* is modern Gk. slang for 'wanker', used affectionately among young men, but to make a connection would be fanciful. Eric Partridge tentatively suggests a connection with modern Gk. *malakia* 'softness'.

Male
C14th. f. L. *masculus* (f. which comes 'masculine', of course). It became *masle* in OFr., and came into Eng. as 'male'. Sp. *macho* went a step further, and meant 'virile' and led to 'macho' and then 'machismo', C20th. The same root is underneath 'mallard', C14th., 'male duck'.

Mama
C16th. it may simply be f. the sound uttered by children on their mother's breast; but note L. *mamma* 'breast', which is widespread in different forms all over Europe. Irish and Welsh have *mam*. Lithuanian – the language that Simeon Potter says is the closest we can get to IE. – has *mama*. 'Mammary', C17th., to mean the breast in animals, comes f. the L. word. 'Mammal', C19th., denotes an animal that suckles its young. The syllable *ma* ramifies widely in the IE. family of languages.

Mammon
C16th. f. the Gk. translation of Mt. 6.24 of Aramaic *mamona* 'riches'.

Man
OE. Orig., this Germanic word meant 'human being' (as does ModGer. *Mensch*); and *wer* (as in 'werewolf') and *wif* (obviously our 'wife') were the words identifying gender.

Manage
C16th. This word has nothing to do etymologically with the previous. It comes f. L. *manus* 'hand' (the meaning is clear in 'manual', C15th., and in 'manicure', C19th). The word had connotations of horse management (It. *maneggiare* 'control a horse') until it took the meaning of 'handling affairs'. Other 'man-' words with this root include 'manipulate', C19th., and even 'masturbate', C17th., f. L. *manu stuprare* 'defile with the hand'.

Mandala
Prob. C20th. Sanskr. 'circle'.

Mandarin
C16th. f. Port. and before that Sanskr. *mantrin* 'councellor'. This word meant a high-ranking bureaucrat in the Chinese empire. The fruit

got its name, C19th., because its colour was the same as a mandarin's robes.

Mangelworzel
C18th. Although to our ears the word is associated with comic stage West Country folk, it is Ger. *Mangol*+*Wurzel* 'beet' and 'root'.

Mango
C16th. f. Tamil *mankay* through Port. *manga*.

Mania
C14th. f. Gk. *mania* 'madness'. Later Gk. used it as a word ending, for example, *gunaikomania* 'mania for women', and modern medicine has followed this pattern: as in 'kleptomania', C19th. (*kleptes* 'thief') and others.

Mansion
C14th. to mean 'a place to stay'; only by C19th. 'a stately home'. The latter has obscured the meaning of Jn 14.2: 'In my father's house there are many mansions'.

Manual
>manage

Map
C16th. f. L. *mappa* 'table cloth'.

Marathon
C19th. In 490 BC, a messenger was sent from a town called Marathon to Athens (over 26 miles) to tell the good news of a Gk. victory against the Persians.

Margarine
C19th. Like the name 'Margaret', this is f. Gk. *magaron* 'pearl', presumably because of the quality of 'margaric acid'. There was an earlier Pers. word *murwarid* 'pearl'.

Marijuana
C19th. Amer. Sp., of uncertain origin.

Marmalade
C16th. I heard Michael Caine, the actor, offer the following on TV: it was one of the few things that Mary, Queen of Scots could eat when she was ill. Hence *'Ma'am est malade!'* This is a folk etymology. In fact, it's f. Port. *marmelada* 'quince jam', f. *marmelo* 'quince'. f. Gk. *meli* 'honey' and + *melon* 'apple'. Incidentally, the given name 'Melissa' also has *meli* and means 'honey bee'.

Martinet
C17th. referred to a system of drill devised reputedly by General Jean Martinet.

Martyr
OE. f. late Gk. *martur* 'witness'.

Masculine
C14th. f. L. *masculus* 'male'.

Masochism
C19th. named after the Ger. novelist Leopold Sacher-Masoch (1836–1895) who wrote about gaining pleasure from injury. >sadism.

Mass
OE. to mean >Eucharist, this comes f. the last words of the L. service *Ite, missa est* 'Go, it is the dismissal'. The L. *mittere* 'send away' can be seen behind words like 'dismiss' and 'mission': a missionary is 'sent'.

Massacre
C16th. f. OFr., of unknown origin, through L. *marcellum* = 'butcher's shop'.

Master
OE. f. L. *magister*. 'Maestro', C18th., 'master of art' is It., 'Mistress', C14th., also descends f. the L.

Mathematics
C16th. f. Gk. *mathema* 'something learnt'.

Matinee
C19th. f. Fr. *matin* 'morning'. So why does it mean 'afternoon performance'? Among the social elite, a 'morning call' was a call made in the daytime as opposed to the evening.

Mattress
C13th. f. Arab. *matrah* 'mat', which derives f. *taraha* 'throw'. So a mattress is, etymologically, something thrown on the floor. Hitchings points out that the It. footballer Materazzi, whom Zidane floored in the 2006 World Cup Final, had an appropriate name.

Matzo
C19th. f. Yid. *matse*. Heb. is *massah*. Rumoured story: Marilyn Munroe, bored by this delicacy, said to her new Jewish in-laws (Arthur Miller's parents): 'Is there any other part of the matzo you can eat?'

Maudlin
C16th. to mean 'drunk', C17th, 'tearful', 'sentimental'. f. Ecclesiastical L. *magdalena*. f. the name of Mary of Magdala, the presumed 'sinner' of Lk. 7.37. The suggestion of tears comes from paintings in which this Mary is seen weeping.

Maverick
C19th. f. the name of Samuel Maverick, a US cattle-owner who did not brand his calves.

Mawkish
C17th. 'sick'. C18th., 'sentimental'. f. *mawk* 'maggot'. OIce. has *mathkr* 'maggot'.

Mayday
C20th. The international naval term for 'help me' has nothing to do with the month. It comes f. Fr. *m'aider*, 'help me'. >SOS.

Mayonnaise
C19th. f. the name of the port Port Mahon, the capital of Minorca.

Mediterranean
C16th. f. Latin words *medius* 'middle' + *terra* 'land'. The Mediterranean is a sea in the middle of land; though the original sense may have been 'in the middle of the earth' rather than 'enclosed by land'.

Medium
C16th. f. L. *medium* middle. Thus 'medieval', C19th. (*aevum*, L. 'age'); 'mediocre', C17th., *mediocris* 'of middle height' (*ocris* 'rugged mountain'). The It. branch is *mezzo*, from which Eng. gets 'mezzo-soprano'; C18th, a voice midway between soprano and contralto. (A soprano I know says that a mezzo-soprano is a soprano without what she calls 'any top', and a contralto I know says that a mezzo-soprano is a contralto without 'any bottom'.) 'Mezzanine', C18th., is a floor between two other floors.

Megalomania
>mania. The prefix mega- is Gk., *megas* 'great'.

Melancholy
C14th. f., ult., Gk. *melas* 'black' + *khole* 'bile'. Too much black bile, according to the medieval mind, caused depression.

Melodrama
C19th. This was originally a stage play with music, and it comes f. Gk. *melos* 'song' + >drama. *Melos* also supplies Eng. with 'melody', C13th.

Melon
C14th. f. Gk. *melon* 'apple'.

Memento
C15th. There are two prayers in the Catholic Mass beginning with this word, L. 'remember'.

Mem sahib
C17th. The second part of this term was used by Indians when addressing a European. f. Arab. *sahib* 'friend, lord'. The first part is supposed to represent the Indians pronunciation of 'Ma'am'.

Menhir
C19th. This word for a monumental stone, the kind that Obelix carries about in the Asterix books, is f. Breton *maen* 'stone' + *hir* 'long'.

Menstrual
C16th. f. L. *menses* 'month'.

Menu
C19th. f. Fr. *menu* 'small'; so *menu de repas* 'list of items in a meal'.

Meretricious
C17th. f. L. *meretrix* 'harlot', which is f. the verb *merere* 'make money', 'serve for hire'; thus 'flashy', 'vulgar'.

Mercy
C12th. f. L. *merces* 'payment'. Christianity uses it metaphorically for God's gift of compassion.

Meringue
C18th. Fr., of unknown origin.

Meritocracy
>democracy

Mesmerism, mesmerize
C19th. f. the name of Friedrich Anton Mesmer (1733–1815), the Austrian doctor who induced trance-like states in patients.

Messiah
C16th. f. Aramaic , orig. Heb. *masah* 'anoint'.

Metaphor
C16th. f. Gk. *meta* meaning 'change' and *phor* carrier. So, a 'metaphor' is a 'carrier of change'. In modern Gk., Bryson tells us (1990) a *metaphor* is a van carrying things from one place to another.

Micro-
This Gk. prefix usually denotes 'small', as in 'microcosm', C15th., (*mikro* + *kosmos* 'world'). >macro.

Middle
OE. a Germanic word. OHG. is *mittil*, ModGer. *Mittel*; an IE. root also produced L. *medius*.

Midwife
C14th. f. *mid* 'with' and *wif* 'woman': thus a woman who is 'with the mother' during the birth.

Migraine
C18th. f. Gk. *hemikrania* 'half-skull', presumably because some migraines attack one side of the head. In C14th., the form was *megrim*.

Mile
OE. f. L. *mille* 'a thousand'. A Roman mile was a thousand paces. 'Millennium', C17th., is a thousand years. 'Millepede', C17th., is f. L. *millepeda* 'woodlouse', was a creature that had, it was assumed – I don't suppose anyone counted – a thousand legs.

Milk
OE. Unsurprisingly, this word is very old, and widespread among Germanic languages. Ger. is *Milch*. There is an IE. root, f. which L. gets *mulgere*.

Minx
C16th. This word for a 'pert girl' is of unknown origin, but *Chambers* cites MD. *minnekijn* 'darling'.

Mis-
This prefix, derived through Fr. f. L. *minus*, denotes 'bad', 'wrong' etc. A few examples: 'miscall', C14th; 'miscarry', C14th; 'misfortune', C15th.

Miser
C16th. f. L. *miser* 'wretch'. L. *miserabilis* also led to 'miserable', C16th.

Misogynist
C17th. f. Gk. *misein* 'hate' + *gune* >woman.

Mistress
>master

Mix
C16th. f. L. *miscere* 'mingle', and related to, among others, Iranian *meascaim*.

Moan
C13th. f. OE. *maenan*. Prob. imit.

Mob
C17th. a shortening of L. *mobile vulgus* 'fickle crowd'.

Mobile
C15th. f. L. *movere* 'move'.

Moccasin
C17th. f. Algonquian.

Mole
C14th. To mean 'burrowing animal': f. MLG. *mol*. The meaning 'discoloured spot' is OE., and is a Germanic word: OHG. is *meilin* 'stain'.

Money
C13th. f. L. *moneta* 'mint'. This was a name for the goddess Juno, and also for her temple, where the mint was. So our word goes back to a chief goddess's name. When we talk of people 'making a god of money', we are unwittingly going deep into the root of the word.

Mongrel
C15th. A Germanic word. 'Mingle' and 'among' prob. come from the same root.

Monkey
C17th. of unknown origin. The other Germanic languages have words related to Eng. >ape: Ger. has *Affe*, OE. has *appa*.

Mono-
This prefix is Gk. 'alone, only, single' etc. Some examples: 'monochrome', for example, C17th., (*khronos* 'colour'); 'monogamy', C17th., (*gamos* 'marriage'). In modern times, the prefix is used, with the same meaning, in words like 'monocycle' (Gk. *kuklos* 'cycle').

Monsoon
C16th. f. Arab. *mausim* 'season' through. Port. *moncao* and Du. *moessen*.

Monster
C13th. f. L. *monstrum*, 'divine portent'.

Month
OE. a Germanic word: OHG. is *manod*. The IE. root meant both 'month' and 'moon', so this word is closely related to the next.

Moon
OE. An IE. root meant both 'moon' and 'month', and versions of it are ubiquitous in Germanic languages: Ger. is *Mond*.

Moor
C14th. Orig. 'inhabitant of Mauretania'. f. Gk. *Mauros*.

Moral
C14th. f. L. *mor* 'custom'.

Morbid
C17th. f. L. *morbus* 'disease'.

Mormon

C19th. f. the name of the alleged author of *The Book of Mormon*, which Joseph Smith, founder of the Church of Jesus Christ of Latter-day Saints, is said to have found and translated in 1830.

Morning

OE. as 'morn' – the '-ing' came C13th. – A Germanic word: Ger., Du. and Danish all have *morgen*.

Morris

C15th. The dance's name is a variation of 'Moorish'. >moor.

Moron

C20th. Orig. a technical term for a person with a very low intelligence. Now purely insulting. f. Gk. *moros* 'foolish'.

Mosaic

C16th. f. Gk. *mouseion* 'place of the muses', which Eng. has in >museum. Collages of this sort were used to decorate places devoted to the >Muses. >music. The meaning 'pertaining to Moses', C17th., is coincidental.

Mosque

C14th. f. Arab. *sajada* 'he worships'. The word came to Eng. through Port. and It.

Mosquito

C16th. f. a Sp. diminutive of L. *mosca* 'fly'.

Mother

OE. like >arse, >axe, >brother, >sister, >star and others, a word that goes a long way to an IE. root. It is widespread among the Germanic languages, but also in the non-Germanic ones. OIr., for example, is *mathir*, and the Rom. languages have words descended f. L. *mater*.

Mountain

C13th. f. L. *mons*.

Mouse

OE. This word is present in most Germanic languages – Ger. has *Maus*, for example, and it's present (*mus*) in L., Gk. and Sanskr. The IE. base denoted 'steal'. The Rom. languages have different, and, interestingly, unrelated words, even to each other: Sp. *raton*, It. *topo*, Fr. *souris*.

Moustache

C16th. f. It. *mostaccio*; Gk. *mustak* was 'upper lip'.

Muesli

C20th. f. Ger. *Mus* 'pap', of which the word is a diminutive. It could have been marketed as 'little pap' . . .

Muezzin
C16th. The Pers. and Turkish pronunciation of Arab. *mu'addin*, f. *udn* 'ear'.

Mug
C16th. f. Scand. Norwegian has *mugge* and Swed. *mugg*. By C18th., it meant 'face', probably because pots were often decorated with faces. By C19th., it meant 'fool', probably, again, because those faces often depicted dimwits. By mid-C20th., it meant 'beat up and rob'. Possibly the victim was seen as a mug in the third sense above.

Mugwump
C19th. US. 'great man aloof from politics'. I was told at school that it mant 'fence-sitter' – with his 'mug' on one side and his 'wump' on the other. f. Algonquian.

Mulligatawny
C18th. f. Tamil *milagu* and *tannir* 'pepper water'.

Multi-
This L. prefix always signifies 'much' or 'many'. Thus, 'multilateral', C20th., 'many-sided'.

Mumble
C14th. Common in Germanic languages, the word goes back to OHG. *mammalon* 'stammer'. Presumably imit.

Mumbo-jumbo
C19th. to mean 'foolish talk'. Perhaps f. the Mandingo language *mama* + *dyumbo* 'ancestor'.

Mummy
C17th. to mean 'body embalmed'. f. Arab. *mumiya* 'embalmed body'. Pers. *mum* = 'wax'. For the meaning 'mother' (only recorded in C19th., but much older in speech) >mama.

Murder
OE. An IE. root produced several Germanic words, including this one and Ger., Swed. and Danish *mord*.

Murmur
C17th. f. L. 'hum'. Presumably imit., like Sp. *murmullo* and It. *mormorio* and Ger. *Murmelm*. So the word is everywhere, not just in Romance languages.

Muse
C15th. f. Gk. *mousa*. >mosaic, >museum, >music.

Museum
C17th. 'a home for the muses'. f. L. *museum* 'study', Gk. *mouseion.*
>mosaic, >muse, >music.

Mushroom
C15th. f. Fr. *mousserin* and late L. *mussirio.*

Music
C13th. f. Gk. *mousa* >muse; >mosaic; >museum.

Muslim
C17th. Arab. 'one who surrenders'.

Mystery
C14th. orig. f. Gk. *musterion* 'secret ceremony', which came to Eng.
through L. *mysterium.*

Myth
C19th. f. Gk. *muthos.*

N

Nadir
C14th. f. Arab. *nazir* 'opposite'.

Nag
C19th. Probably Scand.: Norwegian and Swed. both have dialect, *nagga* 'gnaw', 'irritate', and Icelandic has *nagga* 'grumbling'.

Naff
C20th. Of unknown origin, though there are two suggestions: *Collins* says it may be backslang f. the short form of 'fanny', while Ayto and Simpson point out that Sc. has *nyaff*, 'unpleasant person'.

Naïve
C17th. f. L. *nativus* 'native'.

Naked
OE. The IE. root is visible in L. *nudus*, and Lithuanian *nuogas*. It's in most of the Germanic languages (Ger. is *Nackt*).

Namby-pamby
C18th. A sentimental poet of the early C18th, Ambrose Philips, was derided with this name by contemporaries like Alexander Pope. It's based, of course, on his first name. Rhyming hyphenated words are characteristic of English at its most playful: >argy-bargy'; >arty-farty; >hanky-panky. Other constructions like these (thanks to Terri Morgan's unpublished research) are 'boogie-woogie', 'eency-weency', 'fuddy-duddy', 'helter-skelter', 'hocus-pocus', 'hoity-toity', 'hubble-bubble', 'hurly-burly', 'itsy-bitsy' and 'lovey-dovey'.

Name
OE. A brother/sisterhood word as old as IE. It exists in Fr., Ger., It., Sp. Swed., Yid., Gk., Welsh and Russian. Here they all are, respectively: *nom*, *Name*, *nome*, *nombre*, *namn*, *nomen*, *enw*, and *imja*. Eng. gets the word through Ger.

Nanny
C18th. Diminutive of first name 'Ann' (though before that a 'nanny-house' was a brothel).

Napalm
C20th. f. the initial syllables of 'naptha', C19th., 'inflammable oil from coal' and 'palmitic', also C19th., 'acid from palm oil'. Somebody invented this!

Narcissism
C20th. f. the name of a Gk. youth, *Narcissus*, who saw his face reflected in water, fell in love with it, and pined away.

Nark
C19th., as in 'copper's nark': f. Romany *nak* 'nose'.

Nasty
C14th. This word is obscure, but Swed. dialect has *naskug* 'dirty'. *Chambers* suggests that the word comes f. a pejorative L. suffix *aster*: Eng. has >poetaster (C16th.) 'versifier', etymologically, 'nasty poet'.

Natal
C14th. f. L. *nasci* 'be born'. >native, >nature.

Nation
C13th. f., orig. L., *nasci* 'be born' which led to >natal, >native, >nature and others. The Jew Bloom sums up the meaning in Joyce's *Ulysses*, when confronted by the anti-Semitic citizen, who asks him: 'What is your nation?' 'Ireland . . . I was born here. Ireland'.

Nature
C13th. f. L. stem *natura*, f. *nasci* 'be born'. >natal, >nation.

Naughty
f. OE. *naught* = 'nothing'.

Nausea
C16th. f. Gk. *naus* 'ship' and, later, *nausea* 'sea-sickness'. >nautical.

Nautical
C16th. f. Gk. *naus* 'ship', then *nautes* 'sailor', then L. *nauticus*. Related to >navy.

Naval
C16th. f. L. *navis* 'ship', and related to words in other languages. For example, Irish *nau*.

Navel
OE. Unsurprisingly, this word goes back to a distant IE. root, and it's present in Sanskr. *nabhi-* (also 'wheel hub'), OIr. *imbliu*, Gk. *omphalos*

'boss on a shield', L. *umbo*, and most Germanic languages, whence Eng. gets it. The Romance languages have versions of it, too: It. *ombelico*, Sp. *ombligo*.

Navy
C14th. f. L. *navis* 'ship'. 'Navigate', C16th., is f. the same word. >nautical. The 'nave' of a church, C17th., takes its name f. the building's resemblance to an upturned ship upturned. 'Navvy', C19th., is short for a digger of navigational canals.

Nazi
C20th. This word represents the pronunciation of the first part of Ger. *Nationalsozialist*.

Neat
C16th. f. L. *nitere* 'shine'.

Nebbish
C20th. Yid. for 'Someone who, when he walks into a room, you feel someone has just gone out'. Woody Allen's persona, though not his >person.

Necessary
C14th. f. L. *necesse*. *Ne* is a negative, and *cessis* is 'withdrawal'.

Neck
OE. An IE. base produced, among other words, OIr. *cnocc* 'hill'. Eng. gets it f. Ger. The modern sense, 'caress intimately', C19th., is Northern Eng. dialect.

Negus
C18th. This mulled wine, with cloves, cinnamon, nutmeg, citrus peel and lime juice, familiar to readers of Dickens, was named after its inventor Francis Negus (d. 1732).

Neighbour
OE. formed f. *neah* 'near' and *gebur* 'peasant'. A Germanic word: Ger. has *Nachbar* and Du. *nabuur*.

Nemesis
C16th. The goddess of retribution, f. Gk. *nemesis* 'righteous indignation'.

Nephew
C13th. Widespread in the IE. family, it comes to Eng. f. L. *nepos*, which meant any younger relative (grandson, for example) as well as having its current Eng. meaning. Eng. also gets the word 'nepotism', C17th., f. the L.

Nest
OE. Widespread in IE. languages (L. *nidus*, OIr. *net*), and OHG. is *nest*. Sanskr. *nida* = 'resting-place'.

Neuro-
This prefix is f. Gk. *neuron-* >nerve; hence 'neurology', C17th., 'study of the nerves'. >logy.

Neuter
C14th. f. L. *ne* + *uter*, the former a negative, the second 'either of the two'.

Never
C12th. f. OE. *ne*, a negative, and *aefre*, 'ever'.

News
C14th. not an acronym f. 'North, East, West, South', as many were taught at school. That is a folk mythology. The word is f. L. *nova*, 'new things'. 'Newspaper' is C17th. 'New' goes back to an IE. root, and is there in nearly every European language, f. Lithuanian *naujas* in the east to Welsh *newydd* in the west, and f. Swed. *ny* in the north to It. *nuovo* in the south. Eng. gets 'novel' (by C17th., to mean 'fiction').

Nice
C13th. f. L. *nescius*, 'ignorant', through OFr. for 'silly'. The *sci* part is the root of our 'science', or knowledge, and *ne* is a negative. But then we get on a roller coaster. Down the centuries, the word has meant: (C13th.) 'foolish'; (C14th.) 'lascivious'; (C16th.) 'delicate, coy, difficult to please, over-particular, requiring great precision, trivial, critical, doubtful, carefully accurate'; (C18th. and onwards) 'dainty', 'delightful', 'agreeable', 'kind'. Two of these meanings can be glimpsed in these sentences: 'That is a nice distinction'; 'What a nice cat'. The rest have disappeared. The word is an exemplar of the way words change in their meanings.

Nickname
C15th. ME., f. *eke* 'additional' and >name, of course. A century later the first 'n' had been transferred f. the indefinite article 'an'. >adder, >apron, >umpire for other examples of this.

Nicotine
C14th. The dubious honour goes to Jacques Nicot, Fr. ambassador at Lisbon, who introduced tobacco to France in 1590.

Niece
C13th. A Germanic word – OHG. is *nift* – with relations in, for example, Sanskr.

Niggard
C14th. prob. of Scand. origin; Swed. has *njugg*, Norwegian *nogg*.

Night
OE. Predictably, this is a very old word. There is an IE. root visible in L. *nox*, Gk. *nux* and in (among other places) Welsh *nos*, which we can see in the traditional song '*Ar Hyd Y Nos*', 'All through the night'.

Nightmare
C13th. 'night' + ME. *mare* 'incubus'.

Nihilism
C19th. f. L. *nihil* 'nothing'.

Nirvana
C19th. In Buddhism, 'extinction of individual existence', f. Sanskr. *nis* 'out' and *va* 'blow'. Not 'bliss', as it is now drifting to mean. Other debased religious words are >charisma, >guru, >karma and >icon.

-nomy
f. Gk. *nomos* 'law'. So 'astronomy', C13th., is the 'law of the stars'. >star, for the first part of the word.

North
OE. A Germanic word, obscure in origin, but in the extinct Oscan-Umbrian language, *netro* (which *Chambers* suggests is a cognate), means 'left', and worshippers praying toward the rising sun would find the north on their left; as indeed do modern Chritian worshippers in most Anglican churches. In many cultures, 'north' and >left (L. *sinister*) have ominous connotations. The northern sides of churchyards – the left as you face the altar – are still frequently gloomy places. >cack-handed.

Nose
OE. f. an IE. base; here are some descendants: L.: *nasus*, Sanskr. *nas*, Slavic. 'nos'. Ger. has *Nase*, and we have 'nose'. Fr. has *nez*, and Sp. *nariz*. It. has *naso*, at least for human noses, preferring *nuso* for animal ones, as we use, probably, 'snout' for pigs. Why that persistent 'n'? Because it is a nasal consonant, perhaps?

Nostril
OE. *nosu* + *thyrle* 'hole'.

Note
The musical word, C13th., and the writing word, C15th., are essentially the same. f. L. *nota* 'mark'.

Nous
C17th. For all that it sounds like modern slang, this word is f. Gk *nous* 'mind, intellect'.

Novel
>news

Nubile
C17th. usually used to describe, lasciviously, a pretty girl, the word means 'marriageable' (not always the same thing). f. L. *nubere* 'take a husband'.

Nude
C16th. f. L. *nudus* 'naked'.

Nuke
C20th. US. short for 'nuclear'.

Numbskull
C18th. f. 'numb' + 'skull'.

Nurse
C16th. f. L. *nutrire* 'nourish'.

Nylon
C20th. An invention from the initial letters of New York and London? So I was told at school. Not so. The makers chose *on* ('cotton' etc) and invented *nyl.*

Nymphomania
C18th. new L., f. *nymphe* + >mania.

O

Oaf
C17th. f. ON. *alfr* 'goblin'.

Oak
OE. A Germanic word: Ger. has *eiche*, Du. *eik*; but there is no clear trace of it anywhere else, and its origin is obscure.

Oar
OE. f. ON. *ar*. As Hitchings (2008) points out, many sea words come to us f. our Viking forbears, and they sound like it too. 'Storm', 'mast', 'sail' (all what he calls 'stately and spacious') and this word, where the roar of the sea is audible, are three examples he quotes.

Oasis
C17th. f. Gk. *oasis*, but with North African roots. Coptic (Egyptian) is *ouahe* 'dwelling place'.

Oat
OE. The word is peculiar to English and of no known origin. ME. had *haver* f. the Germanic word, visible now in Ger. *Haver* 'oats'. (>haversack).

Ob-
This L. prefix denotes 'towards', 'in the way of', 'against'; some examples: 'object', C14th., (*jacere* 'throw'); 'obliterate', C16th., (*littera* 'letter'); 'obsolete', C16th., (*solere* 'be accustomed').

Obese
C17th. f. L. *obesus* 'that which eats itself', *ob* + *esus* 'eat'.

Obituary
C18th. f. L. *obire*, 'go down': a euphemism for death. No-one can face up to it, not even the old Romans. Compare our limp expression 'pass away'. For what sounds like an almost exhaustive collection of euphemisms for death, see Monty Python's 'Dead Parrot' sketch.

Oboe
C18th. f. F. *hautbois*, lit. 'high wood'. 'High', of course, refers to the pitch. Eng. reverted to It. form (as for nearly all musical words).

Obscene
C16th. f. L. *obscenus* 'disgusting, ill-omened'.

Ocean
C13th. f. the name of the Gk. god *Okeanos*, who personified the great river that, the ancients believed, encircled the world.

Octa-
This is f. the Gk. prefix *okta*, and denotes 'eight' as in 'octagon', C17th., 'octopus', C18th. (*pous* 'foot').

Octo-
This L. prefix also denotes 'eight', as in 'octuple'.

Odyssey
C19th. f. Ger. *Odusseia*, f. the name of the Homeric hero *Odysseus*, *Ulysses* in L. and in James Joyce's great book (1922) where Dublin stands in for the Mediterranean Sea.

Oenophilia
C19th. f. the name *Oeno*, Gk. goddess of wine, and this word means love of the stuff (>*philo*).

Ogle
C17th. prob. f. LG. *oegeln* = 'look'.

Ogre
C18th. Fr., of unknown origin.

Oil
C12th. L. *oleum* is 'olive oil', but the Gk. *elaiwa* is 'oil'. By C12th. the word meant any 'viscid liquid'. The word 'olive' did not enter Eng. until C13th.

OK
C19th. US. An abbreviation of *orl korrect*, a mis-spelling, facetiously intended or not, of the semi-literate President Andrew Jackson, is the most likely origin, though Bryson has three other possibilities. The Internet will offer many others.

Old
OE. A Germanic word: OHG., and ModGer., is *alt*. The old Germanic base signified, encouragingly, 'grown up'. It is related to L. *alere* 'nourish'.

Olive
>oil

Ombudsman
C20th. Swed., f. ON. *umbothsmathr* 'administrator'.

Omelette
C17th. f. L. *lamina* 'thin metal plate' f. which we get 'laminate'.

Omnibus
C19th. f. L. *omnibus*, and before that, *omnis* 'all'. The poet William Barnes objected to the use of classical words like this for modern things, and proposed 'folkswain', the latter part of which is a very old word for 'waggon' (see Constable's painting *The Hay Wain*), identifiable in a Sanskr. word *vahana*. >Bicycle, for more of Barnes' obsession with ancient Eng. words as opposed to classical ones.

Onanism
C18th. In Gen. 38.9, Onan 'spills his seed upon the ground' instead of completing sex with his late brother's wife. In a society where the survival of the tribe was so vital, one can see this was considered a sin (is this also one of the reasons for the Old Testament's few but trenchant rules against homosexuality?) The word has come to mean 'masturbation', but it originally meant *'coitus interruptus'*. The American humorist Dorothy Parker kept a budgerigar with the name Onan because it spilled its seed on the ground.

Onion
C14th. OE. was *ynne*, f. L. *unio*, also 'pearl' (and, prob. coincidentally, there is a 'pearl onion'). The word died out, and was re-acquired f. OFr. *union*.

Onomatopoeia
C16th. 'Bang', 'smash', 'crash' and the others. f. Gk. *onoma*, name, and *poieo*, 'make'. So, a word that makes something like the sound it is intended to describe.

Onus
C17th. L. 'burden'.

Opera
C17th. f. L. *opus* 'work'. This is the L. plural, but it is sometimes wrongly assumed to be a feminine version of the word.

Opium
C14th. f. Gk. *opion* 'vegetable juice'.

Optic
C16th. f. Gk. *optos* 'seen'.

Orange
C14th. f. Arab. *naranj* and earlier Pers. *narang*.

Orchestra

C18th. f. Gk. *orkheisthai* 'dance'. The ancient Gk. *orkestra* denotes a place where the dancers performed.

Orchid

C19th. f. Gk. *orkhis* 'testicle' (and 'orchitis' is 'inflammation of the testicle' in modern Eng.) There is a dialect name for a wild orchid, 'ballock's grass'. >avocado for another word with the notion of 'testicle' behind it.

Organ

C13th. f. L. *organum* 'musical instrument'. The Gk. led to 'body part'.

Orgasm

C17th. f. Gk. *organ* 'swell'.

Orgy

C16th. f. L. *orgia*.

Orient

C18th. f. L. *orire* 'rise', as is 'origin', C14th.

Ornament

C13th. f. L. *ornare* 'equip', 'decorate'.

Orphan

C15th. f. Gk. *orphanos*, related to *orbus* 'bereft'.

Orth- or ortho-

These prefixes are f. Gk. 'right, correct'. So 'orthography', C15th., is 'correct (or, more precisely, 'accepted') spelling'. >-graph. 'Orthodox' (*doxa* 'opinion'), C16th., means 'in accordance with accepted meaning'. 'Orthodontics', C20th., is the business of putting wonky teeth straight: (*odontos* 'tooth').

Ostrich

C13th. f. L. *avis* 'bird' + late L. *struthio* 'ostrich' with a Gk. word further back meaning 'sparrow'. Gk. *mega strouthos* was 'great sparrow', therefore 'ostrich'. Some understatement, as Ayto says.

Otter

OE. This Germanic word (Ger. is the same) has an IE. root which led to Gk. *hudros* 'water-snake'.

Ouija

C20th. f. Fr. *oui* + Ger. *ja*.

Ovary

C17th. f. L. *ovum* 'egg'; as, of course, is 'oval', C16th.

Oven
OE. A Germanic word which may be related to Sanskr. *ukha* 'cooking pot' and Gk. *ipnos* 'furnace'.

Owl
OE. A Germanic word which probably developed f. the sound of the bird's cry.

Ox
OE. A Germanic word (OHG. is *ohso*) with a root in Sansk. *uksan* 'cattle'.

Oxygen
C18th. The word was made in France, f. Gk. *oxus* 'sharp' and *-genes* 'making'.

P

Pacific

C16th. ult. f. L. *pax* 'peace'. With a capital, f. MedL. *Mare Pacificum*, Magellan's C17th. name for the ocean.

Paddy

There are three words in Eng.: the rice meaning, C17th., is f. Javanese *pari*. The second, C18th., is a pet form of Irish *Padraig*, 'Patrick', and may be derogatary; the fit of temper meaning, C19th., possibly comes f. the second of these.

Padre

C16th. f. L. *pater* 'father' through Sp., It., Port. *padre*.

Paedo–

This Gk. prefix denotes 'child', though in Gk. it was 'boy'. So 'paediatrician', C20th., is a doctor who specializes in children's illnesses (*iatros* = 'doctor'); and 'paedophile' (C20th.) is the revoltingly inappropriate (>philo) name given to child-molesters.

Paella

C20th., prob. Catalan.

Pagan

C14th. f. L. *pagus* 'country district'. The meaning >heathen may have developed because idol worship continued outside cities after most of the main centres of the Roman Empire had been Christianized; or it may have developed as a dismissive city-dweller's epithet, like 'bumpkin'.

Pagoda

C17th. f. Pers. *butkada* 'idol temple', f. *buk* 'idol' + *kada* 'temple', through Port.

Pal

C17th. Romany, for >brother, mate, and goes back to *bhratar*, Sanskr., 'brother'. It comes to Eng. through Turkish *pral*.

Palaver

C18th. f. Port. *palavra* 'speech'; f. L. *parabole*.

Palindrome

C17th. for example, 'Hannah', 'Bob' etc. Gk. *palin* 'back' and *drom-* 'running'.

Palm

C14th. f. L. *palma*, 'palm of the hand', then Sp., It. and Fr. *paume*. It's related to Gk. *palame*, f. which Irish gets *lam* 'hand'. The word went Germanic languages, including Eng., to mean a kind of tree, presumably f. the resemblance of the leaves to the fingers. 'Palmistry', that dreary deception, is C15th.

Pan

OE. This word is prevalent in Germanic languages. ModGer., for example, is *Pfanne*. In Eng. it has meant 'skull' (the skull is a pan for the brain). The word goes back to L. *patina* 'dish' and earlier Gk. *patane*. The verb 'pan', C20th., 'follow with a moving camera' is another word altogether, short for 'panorama'. >Pan-.

Pan-

This Gk. prefix means 'all' or 'whole'. By C19th., it was a customary political usage as in 'Pan-African', '*all* of Africa'. A 'pandemic', C17th., affects 'all the people' (*demos* Gk. 'people'). 'Panorama' is C18th. f. 'whole view' (*horama* 'see'). A pantheist, C18th., believes that God and the universe are identical (*theos* 'god', and is not to be confused with the Gk. god Pan: the Pantheon, C14th., in Rome, was dedicated to all the gods. 'Pantomime', C17th., is f. Gk. *pantomomos*, an imitator who could mimic anything. >pandemonium, >panic.

Panda

C19th. f. Nepali.

Pandemonium

C17th. The poet John Milton coined this word: 'Pandaemonium, the high capital / Of Satan and his peers' (*Paradise Lost* 1:756). He is using Gk. >pan and *daimon* >demon. By mid-C19th., it meant 'uproar', and no doubt those public school masters using it when entering a noisy formroom – they were well-schooled in the classics – were aware of their hyperbole.

Pander

C16th. f. the name *Pandaro* used by Boccaccio and later by Chaucer and Shakespeare in the story of Troilus and Cressida: a man who passes messages between illicit lovers.

Panic
C17th. ultimately f. the name of the Gk. god Pan (half-man, half-goat) whose presence, seen or not, caused terror; though note that his presence in *The Wind in the Willows* (Kenneth Grahame) is benign. There is no connection with >pan-.

Panjandrum
In 1755 the English actor Samuel Foote wrote a nonsense speech to test the renowned memory of another actor, Charles Macklin. It deserves to be better known, and is given in *The Oxford Dictionary of Quotations*. It includes the lines 'there were present the Picninnies, and the Joblillies, and the Garyalies, and the Great Panjandrum himself . . .' It was, and is, used as a mock-title for any pretended great person.

Panorama
>pan-

Pantheist
>pan-

Pantheon
>pan-

Pansy
C15th. f. OF. *pensee* 'thought'. As poor mad Ophelia says (*Hamlet* 4:5), 'there is pansies, that's for thoughts'.

Pantomime
>pan

Pantry
C13th. f. L. *panis* 'bread' through OFr. *paneterie* 'place for storing bread'.

Papa
C17th. f. Gk. *papas*, a child's word, f. *pater* 'father', and ult., like almost all the words for relations, f. an IE. root.

Paparazzo
C20th. This is f. the name of a photographer in the film *La Dolce Vita* (1959).

Paper
C14th. f. Gk. *papuros*, which denoted some kind of reed, and which is almost certainly f. an Eastern language.

Paprika
>pepper

Para-
This Gk. prefix is cognate with many other IE. prefixes, such as 'fore-' in Eng. and 'pro-' in L. It denotes 'by the side of', 'past', 'beyond', 'subsidiary', 'alteration', 'against', 'wrong'. In the following set of words it is usually easy to see which meaning applies. A parable, C14th., is a story in which a truth exists by the side of the narrative. 'Compare these' it implicitly asks us. In the parable of the sower, for example, 'the seed is the word of God' (Lk. 8.11). A paradox, C16th., (*doxa*, Gk. 'received opinion') goes against what is generally thought. A paragraph, C16th., is f. Gk *paragraphos*, a horizontal line under text where a break occurs.

Paradise
C12th. f. Avestan, a Pers. language, *pairidaeza* 'enclosure'. Gk. *perideisos* took it on to refer to the parks of Persian kings: *peri* = 'around', *deisos* = 'mound'.

Paraphernalia
C17th., to mean 'those things that the law allowed to belong to a married woman'. f. Gk. *para* 'beside' and *pherne* 'dowry'.

Parboil
C15th. This curious word originally meant 'boil thoroughly' and only has its present meaning because of confusion with 'part'. f. MedL. *per-* 'through' and *bullire* 'boil'.

Pariah
C17th. Hindi for a member of a low caste, and by C18th. 'social outcast'. Tamil *paraiyar* is the name of the largest low caste, and means 'drummer' because of the instrument played at festivals.

Parent
C15th. f. L. *parenes* 'parent', f. the verb *parere* 'bring forth'.

Park
C13th. A Germanic word, and can be seen in Du. *perk*. It travelled to MedL. and produced *parricus*; thence into English.

Parka
C20th. f. Aleutuian, a language spoken in islands off Alaska, US: it means 'skin'.

Parliament
C14th. f. OF. *parler* 'speak'.

Parsnip
C14th. f. L. *napus* 'turnip'.

Parson
>person

Passion
C12th. A word with an interesting history, it orig. meant 'suffering', at first the suffering of Christ on the cross. By C14th., it also meant 'amorous feeling', and two centuries later, 'sexual impulse'. f. L. *pati* 'suffer'.

Passover
C16th. The Jewish feast celebrating the Exodus is a translation of Heb. *pesah* 'pass over'.

Pasta
>pasty

Pastern
C16th. This word for a part of horse's foot between fetlook and hoof is f. L. *pastorius* 'to do with a shepherd'. It has an interesting corner in lexicography because the great Samuel Johnson got it wrong, defining it as 'knee'. When asked why, he replied, 'Ignorance, madam, pure ignorance' (Boswell's *Life of Johnson*). This remark of such wonderfully non-prevaricating frankness should be an example to us all, and is the only reason why I have included the word here.

Pasteurize
C19th. f. name of Louis Pasteur (1822–1895) who devised this method of sterilizing.

Pasty
C13th. f. late L. *pasta* 'paste'. In Shakespeare's bloody play *Titus Andronicus* the hero 'makes two pasties' from the flesh of Tamara's vile sons, and feeds it to their mother. One thinks of the Cornish delicacy differently.

Patriot
C16th. through L., f. Gk. *patrios* 'of one's fathers', ult. f. *pater* 'father'; which, like almost all relationship words, goes back to an IE. root.

Pavilion
C13th. f. L. *papilio* 'butterfly'. A tent, the Romans thought, was like a butterfly's wings.

Pavlova
C20th. This sweet was named after Anna Pavlova, the dancer.

Pawn
C14th. f. MedL. *pedo* 'foot soldier'; L. *ped* = 'foot'; ult. f. Pers. *piyada* 'foot'.

Pawpaw
C16th. f. Sp. *papaya* and Port. *papayo*, who brought it back f. the Caribbean *papaw*.

Peace
C12th. f. L. *pax*, as with the Rom. languages: Fr. *paix*, Sp. *paz*. Germanic languages have fr- words: Danish and Swed. *fred*, for example, which Eng. has in the noble given name.

Peach
C14th. f. L. *persicum*, via OFr. *peche* 'Persian'. The origin reflects the fact that this Chinese fruit found its way into Europe via Persia.

Pear
OE. f. L. *pira*, of unknown origin, but prob., like Gk. *apion*, borrowed f. a Mediterranean language.

Pearl
C14th. f. L. *perna* 'leg-shaped'. Some mussels that contained pearls were thought to be leg-like in shape.

Peculiar
C15th. f. L. *peculiaris* 'of private property', which is the meaning in the Bible, 1 Pet. 2.9 (AV): 'Ye are . . . a peculiar people' (the property of God).

Pedant
C16th. f. It. *pedante*, which could also mean 'schoolmaster'. See the pedant/schoolmaster Holofernes in Shakespeare's *Love's Labour's Lost* for the connection personified. The origin of the It. word could be, first, f. Gk. *paideuein*, 'teach'; but the word had meant 'foot soldier': a schoolmaster was always on his feet.

Pedestrian
C18th. f. L. *ped* 'foot'.

Pee
C18th. a euphemism, or a word for young children, for >piss. f. Fr. *pipi*.

Peevish
C14th. of unknown origin, though possibly f. L. *perversus*.

Pelican
OE. f. LateL. *pelicanus*. The earlier Gk. *pelekan* is prob. f. *pelekus* axe, referring to the shape of the bill.

Pelvis
C17th. f. L. 'basin', which is cognate with Gk. *pella* 'bowl', and Sanskr. *palavi* a type of pottery.

Pencil
C14th. f. L. *peniculus* 'brush', f. >penis 'tail', 'penis'.

Penguin

C16th. origin unknown. It has been speculated that it is Welsh *pen gwyn* 'white head', which may have referred to an extinct bird. But the penguin, of course, has a black head.

Penicillin

C19th. modern L. The name of moulds, given because of their brush-like nature. >pencil.

Peninsula

C16th. f. L. *paene* 'almost' + *insula* 'island'.

Penis

C17th. f. L. 'tail'. >pencil. cognate with Gk. *peos* and Sanskr. *pasas*.

Penta-

This Gk. prefix denotes 'five'. So a 'pentagon', C16th., has five angles (*gonos* Gk. 'angle'); a 'pentameter', C16th., has five metric feet (*metron*, 'metre'); The Pentateuch, C16th., comprises the first five books of the Bible (*teukhos* 'vessel', later 'book'); a pentathlon, C19th, is an athletic contest with five events (*athlon* 'prize').

Penultimate

C17th. f. L. *paene* 'almost' and *ultimus* 'last'.

Pepper

OE. The word is in Sanskr. and Gk.: *pippali* and *peperi* respectively. It is widespread in Germanic languages, and ModGer. is *Pfeffer*; though, confusingly, the vegetable is *Paprika*, which is a borrowing f. Hungarian, a non-IE. language, borrowed in turn from Slavic. That goes back orig., though, to L. *piper*, which is also behind pepper.

Per-

This L. prefix can denote any of the following: 'through', 'by', 'by means of' and sometimes 'thoroughly'. 'Perforate', C16th., for example, is *per-* 'through' and L. *forare* 'bore'; in 'perfect', C13th., the second part is f. L. *facere* 'make, do'; 'perfume' C16th. (orig. not a pleasant smell) has L. *fumare* 'smoke': so, 'smoke through'.

Perhaps

C16th. f. Anglo-Norman *per* 'by' + ON. *hap* 'chance'.

Peri-

This Gk. prefix denotes 'around'. So 'periscope', C19th., is an instrument that helps you to look around (*skopein* 'observe').

Peril

C13th. f. L. *periculum* 'risk'.

Perish
C13th. f. L. *perire*, >*per-* + *ire* 'go'.

Permanent
C15th. f. L. >*per-* + *manere* 'stay'. The latter is the root in 'mansion'.

Pernicious
C16th. f. L. >*per* + *nex* 'death, destruction'.

Pernickety
C19th. Sc. of unknown origin.

Person
C13th. An unusual word, in that it prob. comes to us, through L. *persona*, f. Etruscans *phersu* 'actor's mask', and that sense is present in Jung's C20th. usage, where he uses the final 'a', and where it means the 'personality we present in a social sense'. Parson, C14th., is a variant.

Pest
C16th. f. L. *pestus* 'plague'.

Pet
C16th. to mean 'favourite animal', f. Irish *peata*.

Pheasant
C13th. f. the name of the Gk. river *Phasis*, whence the bird (or at least its name) spread to the west.

Phil-, philo-
This Gk. prefix denotes 'lover'. So 'philanthropy', C17th., (*anthropos* 'mankind'); 'philander', C18th., (*andros* 'man'); 'philosophy', C13th,. (*sophia* 'knowledge, wisdom').

-phobia
This Gk. suffix is f. *phobos* 'fear'. A selection follows: 'claustrophobia', C19th. (*claustrum* – L., not Gk. 'cloister'); 'Agoraphobia', C19th., (*agora* 'public space'); 'xenophobia', C19th., (*xeno* 'guest, stranger'). For an astonishing and enlightening list of -phobia words, see Hellweg. He quotes 'metrophobia', 'fear of poetry', which I have witnessed, often, myself, and 'hierophobia', a fear of clergymen, which I have *experienced* myself.

Photograph
C19th. f. Gk. *phos* 'light' + *graphos* 'written'.

Piano
C18th. The original It. was *col piano e forte*, describing an instrument that could play 'both soft and loud'. C19th., the abbreviated version was f. It. *piano* 'soft'.

Pickaxe
C15th. f. OFr. *picois* 'pick'. What most of us feel is the 'obvious' etymology – that the word describes what it does – is an elderly folk etymology. *Axe* is there to represent the second syllable of the OFr.

Pickle
C14th. MLG. is *pekel*, but the origin is unknown.

Picnic
C18th. f. Fr. *picquenique*.

Pidgin
C19th. orig. a jargon, especially used in business, spoken in the Far East. By C20th., it denoted any simplified form of language used for communication between foreigners. f. a Chinese corruption of *business*.

Pie
C14th. to mean food wrapped in pastry; prob. f. 'pie', the earlier name of the magpie, whose nest is, like many a pie, a collection of miscellaneous objects.

Pig
Arrived in ME times as *pigga*, meaning 'young pig'; present meaning, C16th; of unknown origin: the OE. word was 'swine'.

Pigeon
C14th. f. OFr. *pijon* 'young bird'. It may go back to L. *pipiare* 'chirp'; so the Eng. is of imit. origin.

Pike
C14th. The fish's name comes f. OE. *pic* 'pointed object', with obvious reference to the shape of the jaw.

Pilau
C17th., and spelt variously. f. Pers. *pilaw*.

Pilgrim
C12th., to mean 'wayfarer'. C13th. the meaning has become more particular: 'traveller to a religious place'. f. L. *peregrinus* 'foreign'.

Pinafore
C18th. f. 'pin', OE., and 'afore', because the garment was pinned in front of a dress.

Pint
C14th. OF. *pinte*, of unknown origin.

Piss
C13th. f. OFr. *pisser*. It's general in European languages; for example, It. *piscare* and Welsh *piso*. It must be of imit. origin; >pee.

Pity
C13th. f. L. *pietas* 'piety'. Later L. reflected the understanding, not universally understood today in religious circles, that 'piety' involves 'pity'.

Placebo
C18th. to mean an inert substance given medically. f. the Roman Catholic Vespers for the dead, verse 9 of Psalm 114: *Placebo Domino in regione vivorum* 'I will please the Lord in the land of the living'.

Plagiary
C16th. f. L. *plagiarus* 'kidnapper'.

Plaice
C13th. f. L. *platessa* 'flat fish', f. Gk. *platus* 'broad'.

Planet
C12th. f. Gk. *planetes* 'wanderer', f. *planan* 'lead astray'. Ancient observers of the universe noticed that the planets, relative to the stars, changed their positions.

Plastic
C17th., to mean 'moulded, modelled', but by C20th. its modern meaning had arrived with the modern stuff. f. Gk. *plastos* 'mouldable'.

Platonic
C16th. 'to do with the writings of the Gk. philosopher, Plato'; in particular, as in *amor platonicus*, the kind of interest in young men that Gk. philosophers advocated. Though the word has kept it original meaning, since C17th., the word has loosened itself from its etymology, and now means any relationship where sex doesn't happen.

Play
OE. For a word of such wide connotations – drama, music, pleasure – 'play' is of surprisingly obscure origin, only existing at one time or another in Germanic languages; and even in those it has died out.

Plebeian
C16th. The *plebs* were >*hoi polloi*, the riffraff, the great unwashed, of ancient Rome, and since C19th. there has been a similar meaning in English; of unknown origin.

Plonk
C20th. Arrived in the UK. with soldiers returning home from France (World War I). Probably f. the overheard phrase *vin blanc* 'white wine'.

Plough
OE. A Germanic word – Ger. is *Pflug* – which came to Eng. through ON. *plogr*.

Plum
OE. f. L. *plunum.*

Plump
C15th., to mean 'dull'; C16th. to mean 'rounded'. f. MD. *plomp.*
Hitchings writes that the word was first used by Caxton to describe the
Dutch as 'well fed, prosperous and dull'.

Plus-fours
C20th. Not a word on everybody's lips, but interesting: the knicker-
bockers are so called because four inches are added to the material to
produce the overhang.

Plutocracy
C17th. >democracy.

Poem
C16th. This word comes to Eng. through Gk. *poein* 'create' and L.
poema. These words are related to Sansk. *cinoti* 'assemble, build up'.
The idea of 'making' a poem, building it, is at the root of the word,
not the debased fag-end romantic idea of waiting in a trance for
inspiration.

Poetaster
C16th. Not what it sounds it should be, a reader of poems. ModL. for
'inept versifier'. >nasty.

Pogrom
C20th. Russian, f. *gromit* 'destroy'.

Polka
C19th. f. Czech 'Polish woman'.

Poly-
The Gk. prefix *polu* denotes 'many'. Thus 'polygamy', C17th., (*gamos*
'marriage'); 'polyglot', C17th. (*glotta* 'tongue'); 'polymath', C17th.,
(*manthalein* 'learn'); 'polytheism', C17th., (*theos* 'god').

Pomegranate
C14th. f. L. *pomum* 'apple' and *granatus* 'seed'. It's etymologically 'a seedy
apple'. The grenade was so named because it looked like the fruit.

Pomp
C14th. f. Gk. *pompe*, then L. *pompa* 'solemn procession'; so, 'pompous',
C14th., f. L. *pomposus.*

Ponce
C19th. 'pimp', later 'effeminate man'; origin obscure.

Poncho
C18th. S. Amer. Sp. 'cloak'.

Pony
C17th. of obscure origin, but perhaps f. L. *pullus* 'young horse' through Fr. and Sc. *powny*.

Poodle
C19th. Ger. *Pudelhund* 'puddle dog'. Surprising as it may seem, this dog was bred to hunt water birds.

Poor
C13th. f. L. *pauper*, through OFr. *povre*, now *pauvre*.

Pope
C12th. ultimately f. L. *pappas* 'father'.

Poppycock
C19th. orig. US. f. dialect Du. *pappekak*, 'soft excrement'. >cack-handed.

Porcelain
C16th. f. It. *porcellana* 'cowrie shell' (also called 'Venus shell'), a diminutive of *porcella* 'sow'; f. L. *porca* 'sow'. The shells are said to have taken the name f. their resemblance (*Chambers*) to the round shape of a pig's back; or (other sources, including Hoad and Webster) f. their resemblance to a sow's external sexual organs.

Porcupine
C14th. f. L. *porcus* 'swine' + *spinus*.

Pork
C13th. f. L. *porcus* 'swine'. Irish is *orc*. Note that the word for the meat comes through Fr. *porc*, while the word for the live animal is OE. *pigga*. Some writers say that this is socially significant: the Saxons knew the creature, and the conquering Normans knew the meat. Others dispute this.

Pornography
f. Gk. *porne* 'prostitute' + >-graph.

Porridge
C17th. f. Fr. *potage* 'food from a pot'. The change from the 't' to the 'r' sound in the middle of the word has two possible explanations. It was influenced by a now obsolete ME. word *porrey* 'soup'; or the change is like the change from the phrase from 'Get off' to one of Billy Bunter's cries in the Frank Richards stories, 'Geroff!'

Port
OE. 'harbour'; C13th., 'gateway'; C14th. 'opening in the side of a ship'; C17th. 'left side of a ship looking forward'; C17th., 'fortified red wine

of Portugal'. All these are related. The first is f. L. *portus* 'harbour'; the second is f. the related L. word *porta* 'gateway'; the third is f. the name of the Portuguese town from which the wine that so entranced the English aristocracy was delivered. *Oporto* is Port. 'the port'.

Porter
C13th. f. L. *porta*. >port. C18th., the dark beer was so-called because porters drank it.

Posh
C20th. is not, as schoolchildren used to be told, an acronym for 'Port Out, Starboard Home', referring to the shady, more expensive cabins of ships on voyages to India. That is a folk etymology. It is f. 'ha'penny', f. a Romany word for 'half'. As *Collins* says, almost all acronymic etymologies are false.

Post-
This L. prefix means 'after'. So, post-communion, C15th., is after the communion, *communis* 'common'; other examples are 'postprandial', C19th., now barely usable except facetiously (*prandium* 'lunch, meal'); 'postscript', C16th. (*scribere* 'write'). 'Postern', C13th., 'back gate' (*posterus* 'what is behind'), is included here because of Thomas Hardy's lovely use of it: 'When the Present has latched its postern behind my tremulous stay . . .' ('Afterwards').

Pot
OE. of unknown origin, though late L. has *pottus*.

Potato
C16th. f. Sp. *patata*, ult. *batata*, native Amer.

poteen
C19th. This word for privately distilled >whiskey is f. Irish *pota* 'pot'.

Pottage
>porridge

Pour
C13th. of unknown origin, though *Chambers* suggests OFr. *purer*, f. L. *purus* 'pure'.

Powder
C13th. f. L. *pulvis* 'dust'.

Prairie
C18th. f. L. *pratum* 'meadow'.

Praise
C13th. f. L. *pretium* 'price', through OFr. So, to 'praise' is to 'give value'. This word is nothing to do with >pray.

Prang
C20th. of unknown origin, though obviously imit.

Prank
C16th. unknown origin.

Prawn
C15th. of unknown origin. No authority I've seen even suggests a possibility.

Pray
C13th. f. L. *precare* 'plead'.

Pre-
This L. prefix denotes 'before', 'in front of' etc. A few examples among many: 'preamble', C14th., (*ambulare* 'walk'); 'precaution' C17th., (*cavere* 'take heed'); '*predict*', C17th, (*dicere* 'say'); 'preface' C14th., *facere* 'speak'.

Pretty
OE. to mean 'crafty'. By C15th., it has, roughly, its present meaning. f. *proett* 'trick'. Modern Du. pret = 'fun'.

Prevaricate
C16th. the last part of this word is f. L. *varus* 'knock-kneed', so the word means, literally, 'walk crookedly'. C17th., 'deal evasively'. It does not (though it probably soon will) means >procrastinate. Language is in a constant state of change: here is a word caught almost at the moment that it changes.

Prevent
C15th. 'act anticipating something'. C16th. 'hinder'. L. >*pre* and *venire* 'come'. Language is like clouds moving slowly across the sky. You can't always see the changes as they happen. There are two arguments about this: we should resist change, or we should embrace it, which, in the case of this word, we did inside a century. When Anglicans pray using the *Book of Common Prayer* 'Prevent us O Lord in all our doings', they mean, 'Go before us O Lord': 'anticipate our problems', effectively.

Prey
C13th. f. L. *praeda* 'booty'.

Priapism
C17th. 'persistent erection of the penis'. f. the name of the L. and Gk. *Priapus* (*Priapos*) 'god of procreation'.

Price
C13th. f. L. *pretium* through OFr. *pris*, now *prix*.

Prick
OE. A Germanic word of unknown origin.

Pride
OE. *pryte*.

Priest
OE. f. Gk. *presbuteros* 'elder'. But another suggestion takes the word back to L. *praepostus* 'person in charge', f. which Eng. gets 'prevost'.

Prig
C17th. 'Thief' or 'tinker'; C18th. for modern meaning; of unknown origin.

Prim
C18th. f. L. *primus* 'prime'.

Prima donna
C18th. It. 'first lady'.

Prime
C14th. f. L. *primus*, and there are many words that have developed in Eng. Some are: 'primal', C14th.; 'primary' C15th.; 'primate', C18th.; 'primer', C14th.; 'primeval', C17th. (L. *aevum* 'age').

Prince
C13th. f. L. *primus* and then *princeps* (>prime + *capere* 'take'). So, literally a prince 'takes first place', as does a 'principal', C13th. 'Principle', C14th., is f. the same root.

Prism
C16th. f. Gk. 'something sawn' – a reference to the shape.

Prison
C12th. f. L. *praehendere* 'seize'.

Pristine
C15th. f. L. *priscus* 'early'.

Private
C14th. ult. f. L. *privus* 'single'.

Prize
C14th. orig. 'booty', it come f. L. *praehendere* 'seize'. >prison.

Pro- words
There are two common prefixes. One is L., and signifies 'for', 'forward', 'in the place of', 'instead of', 'favouring'. Some examples: a 'pro-consul', C14th., stands in for a consul; 'proclaim', C14th. (*clamare* 'shout'); to 'procrastinate' (*cras* 'tomorrow'). 'Progress', C15th. (*gradus* 'step'); a 'pronoun',

C15th., stands in place of a noun; 'Pro-Irish' etc. is obvious. The second prefix is Gk., and signifies 'before'. A 'problem', C14th., (Gk. *ballein* 'throw') is something thrown before a group for discussion. A 'programme' (>*graph*) is something 'written forth'; 'prophet' (C13th., *phetes* 'speaker').

Profane
C15th. f. L. >*pro* + *fane* 'temple'. Thus the profane is 'outside the temple'.

Promiscuous
C17th. Now the meaning is specifically sexual, but its L. derivation, >*pro-* + *miscere* 'mix', suggests its earlier more general meaning in Eng., 'mingled' or 'disorderly'.

Promise
C14th. L. >*pro-* + *mittere* 'send'.

Prose
C14th. f. L. *prorsus* 'straightforward'.

Prospect
C15th. f. L. *pro-* + *specere* 'look'.

Prosper
C15th. f. L. *prosperus*.

Prostitute
C16th. f. L. *pro-* + *statuere* 'set up for all to see' [for sale].

Protein
C19th. the Du. chemist Gerardus Johannes Mulder (1802–1880) coined this word in Fr., *proteine* f. Gk. *protos* 'first': proteins were of primary importance to the body.

Protestant
C16th. Name given to German princes who protested against a group that denounced the Reformation.

Proverb
C14th. f. L. *pro-* + *verbum* 'word': so, a set of words put forward. This word came to Eng. via OFr. *proverbe*.

Prowl
C14th. ME. *prolle*, of unknown origin.

Prude
C18th. a back-formation f. Fr. *prudefemme* 'good woman', also *prud'homme* 'good man'. For two centuries, the word was only applicable to women.

Prudent
C14th. f. L. *pro-* + *videre* 'see'. The latter can more clearly be seen in the synomym 'provident', also C14th. In this word, the *vi-* part was lost.

Prune
C14th. f. L. *prunum* 'plum'.

Pry
C14th. of unknown origin.

Psalm
OE. ult. f. Gk. *psalmos* 'sound of the harp', through L. Etymologically, a psalm is a song sung to the harp. 'Psalmos' is the Gk. Bible's rendition of the Heb. *mizmor*. 'Psaltery', C14th., comes f. the same source.

Pseudonym
C19th. f. Gk. *pseudo* 'false' + *onuma* 'name'.

Psyche
C17th. f. Gk. *psukhe* 'breath, soul'. So, the following: 'psychiatry', C19th. (*iatros* 'healer'), and 'psychology', C19th. (*logos* 'study'); 'psychopath', C19th., (*pathos* 'suffering'). C20th., 'psychedelic', *delon* 'reveal'.

Pterodactyl
C19th. f. Gk. *pteron* 'wing' and *dactulos* 'finger'.

Public
C15th. f. L. *publicus*.

Publish
C14th. f. L. *publicus*.

Puce
C18th. f. OFr. *couleur puce*, ult. f. L. *pulex* 'flea'. So 'puce' is 'flea-coloured'.

Pudding
C13th. ult. f. L. *botellus* 'sausage' from which, worryingly, we get 'botulism', C19th. Puddings were often savoury dishes like haggis or black pudding wrapped in intestines of animals.

Puddle
C14th. ME. *podel*, f. OE. *pudd* 'ditch'. A very English-sounding word, though OHG. had *Pfudel* (ModGer. *Pfutze*). Fr. does not have word, and makes do with the phrase *flaque d'eau* 'pool of water'. >poodle.

Puerile
C17th. f. L. *puer* 'boy'.

Puke

C16th. A Shakespearean invention: f. 'the infant, / Mewling and puking', in the famous 'Ages of Man' speech in *As You Like It* (2:7). Obviously, of imit. origin.

Pukka

C17th. f. Hindi *pakka* 'ripe'.

Pulpit

C14th. f. L. *pulpitum* 'scaffold' or 'platform'. Many preachers might feel the former is appropriate, and their congregations might feel it should be. The L. was used for a platform over the screen between choir and nave in a major church. Now it means that screen.

Puma

C18th. through Sp. f. Quecha language, Peru.

Punch

C17th. to mean 'mixed drink'. Two suggested derivations: the name suggests the physical effect too much of the thing can have on you. And it's f. Hindu *panch* 'five', the number of ingredients, f. Sankr. *panka* 'five'. The first is obviously a folk etymology, the second now disputed; origin unknown.

Pun

C17th. of unknown origin, though Ayto and *Chambers* suggest that it is a shortened form of *pundigrian*, f. It. *puntiglio* 'quibble'.

Pundit

C17th. f. Hindi, but goes back to Sanskr. *pandita* 'scholar'.

Punk

C16th. 'prostitute' says Hoad, and 'strumpet' says *Webster*, and later a boy used for homosexual purposes in prison. The word was adopted by rock groups, C20th., intent on upsetting Daily Mail views of correct behaviour; of unknown origin.

Pupa

C19th. f. L. *pupa* 'doll'.

Purdah

C18th. Urdu f. Pers. *pardah*.

Pure

C13th. f. L. *purus*, related to Sanskr. *puta*, Middle Irish *ur* 'green', 'fresh', 'new' and Welsh *ir*.

Purple

OE. f. L., but ult. Gk. *porphura*, a shellfish that yielded the dye.

Pusillanimous
C16th. one of the words that I always have to look up, but no longer. It's f. L. *puer* 'boy' + *animus* 'mind'. So literally it's 'boy-minded', as though all boys were cowardly and mean-spirited.

Puzzle
C16th. of unknown origin.

Pygmy
C14th. ult. f. Gk. *pugme*, the length from elbow to knuckles.

Pyjamas
C18th. f. Urdu *pay jama* 'leg clothing'.

Pyramid
C16th. f. Gk. *puramis*; perhaps an alteration of Egyptian *pimar*.

Q

Quad-
This L. prefix denotes 'four'. So 'quadrangle', C15th., (shortened to 'quad'); 'quadbike', C20th.; 'quadruped', C17th., (*pes* 'foot'); 'quadrilateral', C17th. (*latus* 'side'). >quart.

Quack
C17th., of imit. origin; cf. Du. *quakken* and others f. Germanic languages. C17th. to mean 'dodgy doctor': a shortening of the earlier 'quacksalver', f. Du. word now *kwakzalver*. The first part is f. *kwakken* 'prattle', the second f. *zalf* 'salve'. So, a chattering easer of pain.

Quaker
C17th. Members of the Society of Friends were said to quake.

Quality
C16th. f. MedL. *qualificare* through Fr. But the base of the word is the L. *qui* 'who'.

Quantity
C14th. f. L. *quantus* 'how much'; f. the base *qui* 'who'.

Quarrel
C14th. f. L. *querella*, f. *queri* 'complain'.

Quarter
Quart- words denote 'four', and stem f. L. *quattour* 'four': 'quarter', C13th., 'quartet(te)', C18th. Sometimes reduced to 'quat', as in 'quatrain', C16th.

Quartz
C18th. A Germanic word of unknown origin; possibly Slavic, as Polish has *twardy*.

Quay
C14th. this word has Celt. origins: Old Celt. is *kagio*. The present spelling, C17th., comes f. its assimilation of modern Fr. *quai*.

Queen
OE. Goes all the way back to IE. 'gwen', meaning 'woman'. It travelled into a Greek as 'gune', and it is f. that word that Eng. gets 'gynaecology', C19th.

Queer
C16th. possibly f. OHG., *quer* 'oblique'; though first used in Sc., and of obscure origin.

Question
C13th. f. L. *quaerere* 'seek, ask'. 'Query', C17th., is formed f. the same L. word.

Queue
C16th. Orig. a heraldic term for 'tail', it comes f. L. *cauda* 'tail'. By C19th., it meant 'line of people'.

Quick
OE. f. OE. *cwicu* living. This word goes back to an IE. base. In the Apostles' Creed (*Book of Common Prayer*, 1662) it says: '. . . he shall come to judge the quick and the dead'. The original meaning is clear from this, as it in Shakespeare's *Henry V* (2:2) when the king says 'The mercy that was quick [living] in us is dead'. The modern meaning, 'rapid' had already emerged in 13th.

Quid
C17th. 'sovereign', now slang for 'pound'. Of unknown origin, though it may, rather obscurely, have descended f. L. *quid* 'something'. A separate word to mean 'chewed tobacco', C18th., developed f. OE. *cudde* 'cud'.

Quiet
C14th. f. L. *quietus*. Other words that come f. this L. word are 'quit' and 'quite'. The underlying sense seems to be about freedom; from noise, from company.

Quiff
C19th. The word for that tuft of hair, oiled meticulously over the forehead in my Teddy Boy days, is of unknown origin; not, disappointingly, related to Fr. *coiffure*.

Quilt
C13th. f. L. *culcita* 'mattress'.

Quin-
This prefix usually denote 'five', as in 'quintuple', C16th., 'quintet', C19th. 'Quintessence', C15th., meaning 'the most perfect representation of a quality or state' comes f. MedL. for 'the fifth essence'.

Quip
C16th. perhaps f. L. *quippe* 'indeed', said sarcastically.

Quisling
C20th. The Norwegian fascist politician Vidkun Quisling (real name Abraham Jonnson) collaborated with the invading Germans in 1940. Hitler made him a puppet prime minister. He was shot for treason in 1945. So this, one of the less honourable eponymous words, means 'traitor who aids the enemy'.

Quit
>quiet

Quite
>quiet

Qur'an
C18th. f. Arab. *kara'a* 'recitation'. 'Read' would sell the word short: it is the public reading of it that counts.

Quiz
C18th., source unknown. It meant 'odd person' or 'mock'. Later it developed its present meaning, influenced, Ayto suggests, by 'inquisitive', though *Chambers* suggests that it is a tenuous connection.

Quixotic
C18th. means behaving like the hero of Cervantes' novel *Don Quixote*, with high but unreachable aims. Cervantes took the name f. Sp. *quixote* 'armour for the thigh', which came, ultimately, through Catalan *cuixa* 'thigh', f. L. *coxa* 'hip'.

Qwerty
C20th. The name of the keyboard arrangement that we all use when writing, named from the first six letters on the top line.

R

Rabbi
C14th. Hebrew, 'my master'.

Rabbit
C14th. f. dialect Fr. *rabotte*. Du. has *robett*, so it may be of Germanic origin. It was only used for the young of the species. The former general word was 'cony', pronounced 'cunny', and may have dropped away because of a similarity to the obscenity >cunt. See Hughes p. 162 for evidence for this.

Rabid
>rage

Rabies
>rage

Race
There are two unrelated words. C13th., to mean 'rush', goes back to ON. *ras*, but beyond that its origin is obscure; C16th., to mean 'a people', f. It. *razza*, is also of obscure origin.

Racket
There are two unrelated words. For the meaning of a network bat, C16th. f. Arab *rahet* 'palm of the hand', through It. *raccetta*. To mean a disturbance or, today, a scam, also C16th., the origin is obscure, and possibly imit. of a clattering noise.

Radar
C20th. US. This is an acronym: '**RA**dio **D**etection **A**nd **R**anging'.

Radio
C20th. formed f. L. *radius*. The sense here is of spokes, or rays, spreading out from a centre. The word is an abbreviation of 'radiotelegraphy'.

Radish
OE. f. L. *radix* 'radish', 'root', f. which we get 'radical'.

Rag
There are three main unrelated Eng. words. C14th. 'scrap of cloth' goes back to ON. *rogg* 'tuft', but the origin beyond is obscure. C18th., to bully or tease, origin unknown; and the word for one the precursors of jazz, C19th., is a shortening of 'ragtime', which in turn comes, possibly, f. 'ragged time'.

Ragamuffin
C14th. f. ME. *raggi* + MD. *muffe* 'mitten'.

Rage
C13th. f. L. *rabies* 'ferocity'. The name of the dog disease, C17th., is obviously f. the same root, as is 'rabid', C17th.

Rain
OE. This word and its cousins exist only in Germanic languages: ON. *regn* for example, and Ger. *Regen*. Romance languages take their word f. L. *pluvia*.

Raita
C19th. Hindi.

Rajah
C16th. prob. came to Eng. through Port. f. Hindi with roots in Sansr. *rajan* and related to L. *rex* 'king'; we see the last in our 'regal'. >maharajah.

Ram
OE. a Germanic word, and may be related to ON. *ramme* 'strong'. 'Ramble', C17th., is f. the same source, and originally denoted the creature, which has always been associated with male sexual rapaciousness, wandering about looking for sex. See Shakespeare's *Othello* 1:1: '. . . an old black ram / Is tupping your white ewe'.

Ramadan
C16th. Arab. *Ramadan* 'hot month'.

Ramble
>ram

Rap
C14th. imit., like 'clap', 'slap' etc.

Rape
C14th. f. L. *rapere* 'seize'. So also is 'ravish', C13th. The plant name, C14th. is f. L. *rapum* 'turnip'.

Rare
There are two unconnected words: C15th., 'unusual, of merit', is f. L. *rarus*, C17th. The word for 'underdone', is f. OE. *hrer*, of unknown origin.

Rascal

C14th. 'young inferior deer', and by C15th., its modern, now rather dated meaning; prob. through OFr. *rascaille* f. L. *radere* 'scratch'.

Rash

C18th. there's an It. word *raschia*, and an OFr. word *rache*, but the late arrival of the Eng. makes any connection unlikely.

Rasher

C16th. of unknown origin, though *Webster* suggests an obsolete ME. word *rashen* 'cut'.

Raspberry

C17th. >Berry was added C17th., but the first part of the word is a mystery.

Rastafarian

C20th. formed f. *Ras Tafari*, the title and surname of Haile Selassie, 1892–1975, Emperor of Ethiopia. *Ras* = 'chief' in Amharic; *Tafari* = 'to be feared'.

Rat

OE. The creature has been around in Europe since about AD 900, and so has the word. f. Rom. *Rattus:* It., for example, is *ratto*; of unknown origin.

Rattle

C14th. Imit. MHG. has *razzeln*.

Raven

OE. This word is almost everywhere in the Germanic languages – ModGer. has *Rabe* – and it goes back to a root that was imit. of the bird's raucous sound. This was more evident in the root's '*khr-*' beginning. Possibly f. L. *radere* 'scrape'.

Ravish

>rape

Raw

OE. A widespread Germanic word with an IE. root that also produced Gk. *kreas*, Sanskr. *kravi* and OIr. *cru*.

Ray

C14th., 'beam'. f. OFr. *rai*, ult. f. L. *radius*.

Re-

This L. prefix can mean one of many related things: 'backwards'; 'in a contrary way'; 'again'; 'in opposition'. It is rarely difficult to understand what meaning is intended. Here is a short group of such words, of which many exist: 'recede', C15th. (*cedere* 'go'); 'rebel', C13th. (*bellum* 'war');

'redeem', C15th. (*emere* 'buy', 'take', with specific Christian connotations, 'buy back from sin'); 'reduce', C15th. (*ducare* 'lead', 'bring'); 'resume', C15th. (*sumere* 'take'); so 'take up again'.

Reach

OE. a Germanic word: OHG. is reichen. It is possibly connected with Lithuanian *raizytis* 'stretch', which suggests that the word goes back a long way: Lithuanian, Barfield suggests, is the European language closest to IE.

Read

OE. f. Old Saxon *radan* 'advise'. Etymologically, it seems that to read is far more than to scan print. It is to 'discern', 'guess'. Perhaps the sentence that sums this up is the old phrase 'read a riddle'. The word is widespread in Germanic languages: Ger. *Raten* is 'advise', and Old Irish *imradin* is 'deliberate'. Sanskr. is *radh* 'accomplish'.

Ready

C12th. f. a Germanic root meaning 'prepared', which produced, among others, Ger. *Bereit*.

Real

C15th. comes ult. f. L. *res* 'thing', which is related to Sanskr. *ras* 'riches'. The word orig. meant, in English, 'pertaining to things rather than people'. The word 'Real' in, for example, the name of the football club Real Madrid, is a different one, meaning (and related to) 'royal'.

Reason

C13th. f. L. *ratio* 'understanding'.

Reckless

OE. 'Reck' was an OE. word meaning 'care'; of obscure origin.

Rectum

C16th. f. L. *rectus* 'straight'. The rectal intestine is straight compared to the rest of them. A related word, 'rectify', C14th., means 'make straight'.

Red

OE. An ancient word that can be traced back to an IE. root. It's in Gk. *eruthros* and L. *russus* (among others). The Germanic branch produced Ger. *Rot* as well as the Eng. word.

Refrigerate

C16th. f. L. *re-* + *frigus* cold.

Regatta

C17th. A Venetian word, 'race between gondolas', but it had come into Eng. by the time Dr Johnson could write to a friend about looking forward to seeing her at 'the regatta'. The original It. is *riggatore* 'wrangle'.

Reggae
C20th. The name of this music possibly comes f. *rege-rege*, Jamaican Eng. for 'quarrel, protest'.

Regicide
>cide

Regular
C14th. f. L. *regula* 'rule'.

Reign
C13th. f. L. *regnum* 'rule', related to the above.

Rein
C13th. ult. f. L. *retinare* 'retain'.

Reindeer
C14th. f. ON. *hreindyri*, and with no connection to the above.

Religion
C12th. f. L. *religio* 'bond'.

Remember
C14th. f. L. >re- + *memor* 'mindful'. The second part goes back to an IE. base.

Renaissance
C14th. meaning 'revival of learning', f. >re 'again' and Fr. *naissance* 'birth', f. L. *nasci* 'be born'. Often spelt *renascence* (by the Victorian poet and critic Matthew Arnold, for example), probably to emphasize L. root *nasci*.

Rendezvous
C16th., 'a place where troops had to gather', f. Fr. *rendez vous* 'present yourselves'.

Renegade
C16th. f. Sp. *renegado*, f. L. *renegare* 'deny'.

Replica
C19th. f. L. *replicare* 'reply'.

Reptile
C14th. f. L. *repere* 'crawl'.

Republic
C17th. f. L. *res* 'thing', 'matter' + *publicus*. The affairs of a republic are supposed to be managed by the people.

Requiem
C14th. f. L. *requies* 'rest'. The word is the first word of the introit of the L. Mass: *Requiem aeturnam dona eis, Domine* 'Rest eternal grant unto them, O Lord'.

Rest
There are two words. The first, 'sleep', 'kip', 'chill out' is OE. from a Ger. term., and may go back OS. *rasta* 'bed' and OHG. *rasta* 'mile' (you've gone this far, have a rest). It's present in Norwegian *rast* for 'distance after which you need a rest'. The meaning 'remainder', C15th., is f. L. *restare* 'stand'.

Restaurant
C19th., replacing 'tavern', C13th., f. L. *taverna*; f. L. *restaurare* through Fr. *restaurer* both 'restore'. Note that the spelling of 'restaurateur', C18th., is closer to the L. root.

Rhinoceros
C13th. f. Gk. *rhis* 'nose' + *keras* 'horn'. The use of 'rhino' to mean money goes back to C17th. Why this sense exists is unknown.

Rhododendron
>rose

Rhyme
>rhythm

Rhythm
C16th. f. Gk. *rhuthmus*, f. whence it passed through L. into Eng. It orig. meant 'rhymed verse'. Many believe that 'rhyme', C17th., comes f. the same source, but *Chambers* casts doubt on this, and says that the word's origin is uncertain. The word was orig. spelt 'rime', the OFr. spelling and the one that Coleridge chooses for 'The Rime of the Ancient Mariner' (1798). The modern spelling emerged in the C16th, under the influence of 'rhythm', so Coleridge was being consciously archaic.

Rice
C13th. f. ME. *rys*; comes to us, *via* L. f. Gk *oruza*. But as the plant is oriental, the word may have origins in Sanskrt *vrihi-*.

Riddle
OE. A riddle is something you >read or 'discern': that is the OE. meaning of *raedan*.

Ride
OE. widely known in Germ. languages, and also in Celtic ones (*reiten, rida, riadaim* in Ger., Swed. and Irish respectively); but the origin is obscure.

Riffraff
C15th. f. OFr. *rif et raf* 'one and all'.

Right
OE. *riht*, common in Germanic languages, with roots in IE. Gk. is *orektos* 'tall', L. *rectus*, all denoting straightness. >left, which denotes something like the oppostite.

Ring
There are two unrelated words: OE. to mean 'circlet' etc., goes back to a Ger. root; OHG. *hring*; ModGer. is *Ring*, also Danish. The bell's sound is f. OE. *hringan*.

Riot
C13th. f. OFr. *riote*, of unknown origin.

Ripple
C17th. unknown origin.

Risk
C17th. f. Fr. and It. *risque* and *risco*; of unknown origin.

River
C13th. f. It. *riviera* 'river bank', ult. f. L. *ripa* 'bank'.

Road
OE. Mainly used for 'raid' (cf. modern 'inroads', C16th.) and later 'sheltered water where ships could be held at anchor'. Its present meaning is C16th; a Germanic word.

Roast
C13th. f. OFr. rostir. f. a W. Ger. word for 'cooking grid'.

Rob
C13th. f. OFr. *robber*, f. a Ger. base meaning 'break'.

Robin
C15th. f. the given name 'Robert'. The bird was called 'robin redbreast' till C16th.

Robot
C20th. unusually, f. Czech: *robota* 'work' or even 'forced labour', related to Ger. *Arbeit*. The Old Slavic *rabu* 'slave' is traceable to an IE. root.

Rock
C14th. to mean 'solid part of the earth's crust', f. OFr. *roche*; origin unknown.

Rogue
C16th. f. a form of *roger* (with a hard 'g'), a beggar pretending to be an Oxbridge scholar; perhaps f. L. *rogare* 'ask'. The word for an elephant

living away f. the herd, C19th., may be f. the same source, but it also might be f. Sinhalese *hora*, f. Sanskr. *cora* 'thief'.

Romantic
C13th. 'romantic', unsurprisingly, stems f. 'Rome'. The word has travelled, though: 'romance' stories involved chivalry, and this has led to the modern meanings. 'Romantic' art (to over-simplify shamelessly) depends on expressing feelings, rather than purely classical notions of order etc., and a modern 'romantic novel' takes its name f. a debased form of that meaning.

Roof
OE. a Scand. word. which has passed into the Germanic languages. ON. has *hrof* 'boatshed', and so has Old Frisian, a language that many authorities say has much in common with OE. Danish has *roef* for 'coffin lid', which says something about Scand. life pre-1000 AD.

Rook
OE. ON. has *hrokr*. The Gk. root is prob. of imit. origin.

Room
OE., to mean 'space': Ger. has *Raum* 'space'. By C15th., the modern meaning emerges.

Rose
OE. f. L. *rosa*, which led to many European words; prob. f. Gk. *rhodon*, which led to our 'rhododendron', C17th. (*dendron* 'tree').

Rough
OE. widespread in Germanic languages – MLG. is *ruch*; this word can also be seen in Lithuanian *rukti* and Sanskr. *ruksa*. 'Ruffian', C16th., is not related, coming f. dialect It. *rofia* 'scab', and *ruffiano* 'pimp'. Its English meaning, not as pejorative as the It., was prob. influenced by 'rough'.

Round
C13th. f. L. *rotundus*.

Rover
C14th. f. MD. *roven* 'rob'.

Royal
C14th. f. L. *regalis*.

Rub
C14th. origin unknown, though there is a LG. word *rubben*.

Rubbish
C14th. f. Anglo Norman *rubbous*, of unc. orig.

Ruby
C14th. f. L. *rubeus* 'red', f. which Eng. gets 'rubicund'.

Ruffian
>rough

Rugby
C19th. f. the name of the English public school where, so the legend goes, a boy picked up the ball in a game of association football and ran with it, thus inventing a new football code.

Rum
C17th., of unknown origin but prob. a shortening of *rumbullion*.

Rumba
C20th. Cuban Sp., f. *rumba* 'spree'.

Ruthless
'Ruth' is C12th. word for pity, coming f. OE. *rue*, with OldGer. roots.

S

Sabbath
OE. ult., f. Heb. *sabath* 'rest', whence into Gk. and L.

Sad
OE. a Germanic word – OHG. is *sat* – with an IE. root present in L. *satis* 'enough'. Etymologically, to feel sad is to feel that one has had enough.

Sadism
C19th. f. the name of the Fr. Count (though he was called Marquis) de Sade (1740–1814), with reference to his crimes and his writing.

Safe
C13th. f. L. *salvus* 'unhurt', and is related to Gk. *holos* and Sanskr. *sarva*. This word assimilated 'save', C15th., which was the earlier spelling of the name of the place where one keeps things secure.

Sag
C15th. prob. of W. Scand. origin, as are, unsurprisingly, many nautical words: they came with the Vikings. Its first meaning was 'drift' in the sea-faring sense. It has cousins in Danish and Norwegian.

Saga
C18th. Icelandic, the word meaning 'saying', 'proverb'.

Sahib
>memsahib

Sail
OE. has a Germanic source, but beyond that it is of unknown origin.

Saint
C14th. f. L. *sanctus* 'sacred'.

Salad
C15th. Many 'sa' words have the root *sal*, L. >salt, in common. Romans kept their raw vegetables in salt, and called the dish *herba salita*, salted vegetables.

Salary
C14th. f. L. *sal* 'salt'. A Roman soldier was paid in salt (see above), which was precious because it kept food fresh.

Salmon
C13th. f. L. *salmo.*

Salt
OE. f. *salsus* 'salted'. The word is present in many languages deriving f. IE., which is not surprising, as the stuff must have been a necessity throughout the world. OIr., for example, is *salaan.* >salary. 'Sausage', C15th., is f. the same L. root.

Same
C12th. f. an IE. root, whence come Gk. *homo*, OIr. *som* and many others.

Samphire
C16th. The harvesting of this cliff plant was a 'dreadful trade' according to Edgar in Shakespeare's *King Lear* 4:5. f. Fr. [*herbe de*] *Saint Pierre.*

Sandal
C14th. f. Gk. *sandalion*, through L., and prob. f. an Asiatic root.

Sandwich
C18th. The fourth Earl of Sandwich (1718–1792) was so addicted to gambling that he would only eat meat between slices of bread while at the gaming-table.

Sarcasm
C16th. f. Gk. *sarkazein* 'tear flesh'.

Sardine
C15th. f. L. and Gk. *sarda*, prob. connected to the island of Sardinia.

Sardonic
C17th. Again, here is Sardinia, where a plant grew which, according to the Ancient Greeks, produced facial contortions resembling bitter laughter.

Sari
C18th., though then spelt 'saury'. Hindi *sahri.*

Sassenach
C18th. A usually derogatary term for the Eng., it comes ult. f. L. *Saxones* 'Saxons'. The Sc. is *Sassunoch*, the Irish *Sasanach*, the Welsh *Seisnig.*

Satan
OE. f. Heb. through Gk. and L. 'enemy, plotter'.

Satin
C14th. f. Arab. *zaituni* 'pertaining to Tseutung', a town in China, the port from which the material was exported.

Satire
C16th. f. L. *satira* 'medley of verses'.

Sausage
>salt

Sauté
C19th., meaning 'fried'. f. L. *saltare* 'jump': you toss the food as you sauté it.

Savage
C13th. f. L. *silva* 'wood', via OFr. *sauvage*. A savage was orig. someone from the countryside rather than the city. >Pagan has a similar story.

Saveloy
C19th. f. It. *cervello* 'brains', which in turn comes f. L. *cerebellum*, which, of course we have in Eng. to mean that part of the brain that controls balance and muscular co-ordination. Who'd have thought that your spicy banger and your physical balance could be connected?

Saxophone
C19th. The name of the instrument comes f. its inventor's name, Antoine Joseph Sax (1814–1984), whose father Charles Joseph Sax (1791–1865) invented the less well-known saxhorn.

Scam
C20th. to mean 'swindle', US., of unknown origin.

Scamp
C16th. f. L. *ex-* + *campus*. A scamp is etymologically one who runs away from the battlefield.

Scampi
C20th. plural of *scampo* 'a kind of lobster'; a Venetian word.

Scandal
C16th. f. Gk. *skandalon* 'snare for an enemy', and is related to Sanskr. *skandati* 'jumps' and L. *scandere* 'climb'. It orig. meant 'act by a religious person that was a discredit to religion'. 'Slander', C13th., is etymologically the same word.

Scatology
C19th. f. Gk. *skor* 'dung' + *-ology* ('study').

Scent
C14th. f. L. *sentire* 'perceive'. Orig. *sent*, the modern spelling is C17th.

Sceptic

C16th. The followers of the Gk. philosopher Philo of Elis took their name f. Gk. *skeptesthai* 'look about', 'consider'. So the sceptic thinks before making a commitment.

Schizophrenia

C20th. f. Gk. *skhizein* 'split' and *phren* 'mind'. This does not mean 'being in two minds about something'.

Schlock

C20th. Prob. a US. Yid. borrowing f. Ger. *Schlacke* 'dregs, rubbish'. As with most of these 'sch-' words (and there are few coming) this has been brought into English (mainly US.) by Jewish emigrants f. Middle Europe, of whom, Hitchings suggests, there were over two and a half million around the turn of C19th. and C20th. Hitchings says that Yiddisher scholars prefer the spelling 'sh-' to the Germanic 'sch-'. This word means 'inferior stuff'.

Schmaltzy

C20th. 'sentimental', mostly US., f. Yid. *schmaltz* 'melted fat', also in MHG. *smelz*.

Schmooze

C19th. 'to talk idly', f. Yid. *shmuesn* 'chat', f. Heb. *shemuoth* 'news, rumours'.

Schmuck

C19th. 'idiot'. f. a Yid. taboo word for 'penis'. Why slang words for this organ become insults ('prick', for example, and 'cock up') is still open to question. 'Balls', to mean rubbish, is interesting too. Though the most powerful insult is still >cunt, though that is an area for psychologists.

Other C20th. words in this Yid./US. Eng. category include *schmutter* 'clothes material', *schlep* ('traipse' would be a near equivalent) and *schtum* 'silent'.

School

OE. Widespread in Germanic and Rom. languages (Fr. *ecole*, It. *scuola*, Welsh *ysgol*, Irish *scoil*) the word comes, through L. *schola* f. Gk. *skhole*, which was orig. a place of leisure.

Science

C14th. 'knowledge'. f. L. *scientia*, f. the verb *scire* 'know'. The modern more particular meaning is C18th, and even when the Victorian public schoolmaster John Addington Symmonds wrote his hymn 'These things shall be', the third line, 'with light of science in ther eyes', did not exclude the boys reading Latin and Greek.

Scissors
C14th. f. L. *caedere* 'cut'. The additional 's' emerged C16th. by assimilation with *scindere* L. 'cut'.

Scoff
C14th. perhaps Scand. Early Modern Danish has *skuf* 'joke'. The word is cognate with OE *scop* 'poet'.

Scold
C13th. prob. f. ON. *skald* 'poet'. There is a special place in Icelandic poetry for material that mocks – *Skaldskapr* = 'poetry that libels'.

Scoundrel
C16th. of unknown origin.

Scouser
C20th. f. *lobscouse*, a sailor's stew.

Scowl
C14th. of Scand. orig: Danish is *skule* 'look downwards'.

Scratch
C15th. The origin is obscure, but Germanic languages have similar words. Ger., for example, is *Kratzer*.

Screw
C15th. f. ult. (there are many Germanic words) L. *scrofa* 'female pig'. This may be because of the creature's curly tail. W. Ger. has *scruva* and OFr. *escroue*.

Scribe
C14th. f. L. *scribere* 'write', 'copy'. An IE. base can also be seen in Gk. *skariphastai* 'scratch'. 'Scribble', C15th., is f. the same root, and so is 'script', C14th.

Scrotum
C16th. f. L. *scrautum*, which was a sheath made of skin containing arrows. 'Arrows of desire' as the poet William Blake puts it in a poem sung as the hymn 'Jerusalem' by Middle England; sung presumably, in all innocence.

Scrounge
C20th. f. dialect 'scrunge'.

Scrumptious
C19th. US., and of unknown origin.

Scuffle
C16th. f. Scand., Swed. *skuffa*.

Sculduggery

C19th. US. of unknown origin There is an earlier word, 'sculduddery', C18th., which Hoad says is Scand., and which means 'fornication'.

Sculpture

C14th. f. L. *sculpare* 'carve'; an Eng. descendant of this L. verb is 'scalpel'.

Scum

C13th. The IE. root denotes 'covering', and the word is in most Germanic languages. Ger. is *Schaum*. The meaning 'dirt', and subsequent insulting usages, are C20th.

Se-

This L. prefix denotes 'without', 'apart', etc. So 'secede', C18th., is 'go apart' (*cedere* 'go'); 'secret', C14th., is 'keep apart' (*cernere* 'separate'). A 'secretary', C14th. 'keeps apart, secret, (C14th.)' his or her boss's secrets. Ayto quotes a beautiful example of the last word: '[Christ] taking with him his three special secretaries . . . Peter and James and John'. (Nicholas Love *Mirror of the Life of Jesus Christ* 1400).

Sea

OE. The word is widespread in Germanic languages – Ger. is *see*, but its origin is unknown.

Search

C14th. If you mislay your keys and find you are going round in circles looking for them, you are close to the etymology of this word, which is f. L. *circare* 'go round'.

Season

C13th. f. L. *satio* 'act of sowing'. Later the word came to denote 'any suitable time', and by C14th., it had its current meaning.

Second

C13th. f. L. *secundus* 'following'. The meaning 'a sixtieth of a minute' comes f. L. *secunda minuta*.

Seed

OE. a Germanic word, and its IE. root has produced many English words, such as 'semen', C19th., and 'disseminate', C17th.

Semi-

This prefix is L. for 'half' or sometimes 'partly'. It's a cousin of Gk. *hemi-*. Some examples are 'semicircular', C15th. (L. *circularis*); musical terms like 'semibreve', C16th., and 'semiquaver', C16th.

Semite

C14th. This name for the Hebrew and Arab races come f. the name of Noah's son, Shem (Gen. 10).

Senile
C17th. This word and 'senior', C14th., come f. L. *senex* 'old man'. The word goes back to an IE. root, which is also behind Welsh *hen* 'old'.

Sense
C14th. f. L. *sensus*, 'feeling'.

Sentence
C13th. f. L. *sententia* 'opinion', 'thought'.

Sept-
This L. prefix denotes 'seven'. So a 'septet', C19th. is a musical piece for seven instruments.

Serenade
C17th. This 'song for the night' is f. It. *sereno* 'serene', possibly influenced by *sera* 'evening'.

Serene
f. L. *serenus* 'calm'.

Serendipity
C18th. Coined by the novelist Horace Walpole (1717–1797), this word is f. *Serendip*, an old word for Sri Lanka, which in turn comes f. Arab. *Sarandip*.

Sergeant
C12th. to mean 'servant', f. L. *servire* 'serve'. The word did not mean 'non-commissioned officer' until C16th. So 'that fell sergeant death' is a servant (*Hamlet* 5:2).

Serious
C15th. f. L. *seriosus*. Beyond that, the origin is obscure.

Servant
C13th. f. L. *servire* 'serve'.

Sex
C14th., as in 'the male sex'; to mean 'sexual activity', C20th. f. L. *sexus*.

Shabby
C17th. OE. *sceabb* f. ON. root. *Skabbr* 'scab'.

Sham
C17th. of uncertain origin, but possibly a variation of 'shame', OE., which is a Germanic word. 'Shamefaced', C16th., is nothing to with 'face'. The second part denotes 'fast, firm'. So, the word means 'held firm by shame'.

Shambles
C15th. dialect. Orig 'meat-shambles'. The second part comes f. OE. *sceamul* 'stool', 'table'. Presumably the Shambles in York, once a meat market, and now said to be the oldest medieval street still intact in Europe, was a rowdy place on market day.

Shame
>Sham

Shampoo
C18th. f. a Hindi word meaning 'massage'.

Shamrock
C16th. f. Ir. *seamrog*, f. *seamar* 'clover'.

Shanty
C19th. f. Fr. *chanter* 'sing'.

Shark
C16th. of unknown origin. The origin of the word meaning 'swindler', also C16th., is obscure too.

Shawl
C17th. prob. through Pers. *sal*, f. the name of a town in India, Shaliat. The word has spread into other European languages, for example, Fr. *chale*.

Sheep
OE. Widespread in Germanic languages – Ger. is *Schaf*, for example – but with no cognates, not even in Scand.

Sheikh
C16th. f. Arab. *saik* 'old man'.

Shelter
C16th. of unknown origin.

Shemozzle
C19th. 'muddle'. f. Yid. *shlim* 'bad' + *mazel* 'luck'.

Shenanigan
C19th. f. Gael. *sionnachuighim*. Well, so I thought, and so says Bryson. But *Chambers* says the word is US., and of uncertain origin, and suggests that Sp. *chanada* 'trick' may be the source.

Sherry
C16th. f. the name of the town where it was first made, Jerez de la Frontera, orig. *Xerez*.

Shibboleth
C17th. This word, 'stream' in Hebrew, was used by Jephthah to smoke out his enemy the Ephraimites who could not pronouce 'sh': they said

'sibboleth' and had a brutal end. (Judg. 12.4–6). Now it means a tired political slogan.

Shiite
C18th. f. *Shiah*, and further back Arab., *sa'a* 'follow'.

Shillelagh
C18th. f. the name of a village in Wicklow, Ireland, which was famous for its oaks, f. which the cudgel was made.

Shilly-shally
C17th. meaning to dither, this word derives f. 'Shill I go or shall I stay?'

Shin
OE. A Germanic word (Ger. is *Schienbein*) meaning 'thin plate'.

Ship
OE. f. OHG. *skif.* The word has a Germanic root, but beyond that the origin is obscure.

Shirt
OE. f. ON. *skyrta*, based on a Germanic word meaning 'short'. 'Skirt', C13th., is etymologically from the same word.

Shit
C17th. This Germanic word is present in many northern languages, for example, ON. *skita*. The IE. root meant 'divide' (>*turd*) so the idea is of waste material separating itself from the body.

Shoe
>slipper

Shogun
C17th. a Japanese title, but ult. f. Chinese *chian chung* 'military leader'.

Shop
C13th. f. Germanic *schopf*, through OFr. *eschoppe*. In the C16th., the verb came to mean 'imprison', an ancestor, presumably, of our meaning 'inform against'.

Shoulder
OE. a Germanic word: Ger. is *Schulter.* Beyond that, of obscure origin.

Shout
C14th. of uncertain origin, but perhaps f. a Germanic base meaning 'project', 'send forth'.

Shower
OE. a Germanic word, and ON. is *skur.* Beyond that, little is known.

Shrapnel

C19th. The shell that bursts and scatters bullets was invented by Henry Shrapnel (1761–1842). Along with >Quisling and >Nicotine, this is one of the less creditable eponyms.

Shrimp

C14th. related to MLG. *schrempen* 'shrivel'. The meaning 'puny person' is of almost the same date; this is unusual, as most metaphorical meanings emerge after the primary one.

Shrivel

C16th. Possibly f. Swed. dialect *skryvla* 'wrinkle'.

Shy

OE. There is a pre-Germanic root meaning 'afraid'. No definite connection has been made between this adjective and the word meaning 'throw', C18th.

Sibling

C20th. a revival of an OE. word, cognate with many Germanic words: Old Frisian is *sibbe*.

Sick

OE. This is a Germanic word, but its roots are obscure. A boy in a classroom said to me, after a story he'd enjoyed, 'That's sick'. It meant 'very good'. >wicked. Is this another word we can see changing before our eyes? Or ears? Perhaps the boy's meaning won't have the strength to stay around. It's an example of the subversion of a word. Homosexual activists reclaimed the aggressive word 'queer', and now there are departments of Queer Studies in Universities. Something of the same has happened with 'nigger'.

Sideburns

C19th. US. named after a wearer of them, General Ambrose E. Burnside (1824–1881).

Siesta

C17th. f. Sp., of course, but the Sp. comes f. L. *sexta hora* 'sixth hour', which was midday to them when they (well, the upper classes anyway) took a nap.

Sight

OE. a Germanic word. Ger. is *Gesicht*.

Sign

C13th. Through OFr. *signe*, this comes f. L. *signum* 'mark'.

Sikh

C17th. A Hindi word related to Sanskr. *siksate* 'learns'.

Silence
C13th. f. L. *silentium*.

Silhouette
C19th. Etienne de Silhouette (1709–1767) was a Fr. politician with financial responsibility and a reputation for parsimony, and word came to mean 'something skimped'. Perhaps this artform reflects that in its lack of paint etc., or perhaps the man himself made such pictures.

Silk
OE. f. Gk. *Seres*, an oriental people from whom silk was passed through Slavonic countries. Old Slavic is *selku*, and L. has the word. So has OIr., *siric*.

Silly
C15th. This is one of those words – like >nice and >gay, among many others – that has travelled far. Its Ger. cousin, *selig*, still means 'happy, blessed', and that is what 'silly' meant in English a thousand years ago. The meaning changed, through 'pious' and 'weak', till it arrived at its present meaning. The county in which I write this was known as 'silly Suffolk', because for some reason it was seen as a particularly devout county.

Silver
OE. A Germanic word, though there is, perhaps, an Assyrian source, *sarpu*.

Simian
C17th. f. L. *simian*. *Simus* was 'snub-nosed', and came f. Gk. *simos*. There is an IE. root.

Similar
C17th. f. L. *similaris* based on an IE. root meaning 'same'. Simile, C14th., is f. the same root.

Simmer
C17th. An alteration of 'simper', of imit. origin.

Simple
C13th. f. L. *simplus*. There is an IE. root.

Simultaneous
C17th. f. L. *simul* 'at the same time'.

Sin
OE. There is a prehistoric Germanic root which produced cognates like Ger. *Sunde*, f. which the Eng. word came.

Sincere
C16th. f. L. *sincerus*. >Introduction.

Sing
OE. a Germanic word (modern German is *singen*), perhaps related to Gk. *omphe* 'voice'.

Single
C14th. f. L. *singulus*.

Sinister
C15th. f. L. *sinister* '>left', which could also mean 'awkward, unlucky'. There have always been suggestions of ill-luck about the left side of the body. As recently as the early C20th., left-handed children were taught to write with the right hand, sometimes with ill effects on the child's well-being, much as churchyard to the left of an old church (as you face the altar), the North side, was believed to inhabited by bad spirits. Even today, many northern parts of churchyards are vaguely disturbing places.

Sinn Fein
C12th. Irish: 'we ourselves'.

Sir
C13th., when the word was only applied to real knight, or at least to a superior male. Now simply respectful, it is a shortening of 'Sire', which in turn comes f. L. *senior*.

Sirloin
C16th. f. OFr. *surloinge* 'upper part of a loin of beef': *Sur* = above, *loin* = 'limb'. A folk etymology, one of the most persistent and ridiculous, says that it was named by a king – Henry VIII and Charles II are often cited – who enjoyed it so much that he knighted it.

Sister
OE. There is an IE. root, and its descendants are many. There is L. *soror*, for example, Fr. *soeur*, and It. *sorella*. Serbo-Croat is *sestra* and Welsh *chwaer*.

Sitar
C19th. f. Old Pers. *si* 'three' and *tar* 'string'.

Sizzle
C17th. of imit. origin.

Skate
C14th. (the fish) f. ON. *skata*.

Skedaddle
C19th. of unknown origin.

Skeleton
C16th. f. Gk. *skeletos* 'dried up'.

Ski
C19th. f. Norwegian *scio* 'snow-shoe'.

Skill
C12th. It orig. meant 'reason, discernment'. By the following century it meant 'practical knowledge', which is the definition that we have today. f. ON. *skil* 'discernment, knowledge'.

Skin
C11th. f. a Germanic word, related to ON. *skinn*. As a verb, the underlying sense is of taking off a cover.

Skipper
C14th. f. Du. *schipper* 'ship's captain'. f. *schip* 'ship'.

Skirt
>shirt

Skull
C13th. The Anglo-Saxons used the resonant *headfodpanne* 'headpan', but this word took over. Origin uncertain, but Norwegian has *skalle*, so it is likely to have come with the Vikings.

Skulk
C13th. f. Scand. languages, for example, Norwegian *skulka*.

Sky
C13th. ON. *sky* meant 'cloud'. 'Sky' had been *heofan* to the Anglo-Saxons. There is an IE. base meaning 'cover'.

Slander
>scandal

Slang
C18th. Origin obscure, but some have suggested a relationship to Norwegian dialect *sleng* – 'offensive language'.

Slave
C13th. f. L. *Sclavus* 'Slavic', and is the result of that race being subjected to servility.

Sleep
OE. a Germanic word: Ger. is *Schlafen*.

Slender
C15th. of unknown origin.

Slim
C17th. It was not always a compliment to be called this, because in MD. it meant 'slanting, bad'. A Germanic word.

Sling
C13th. f. ON. *slyngva*.

Slip
C13th. to mean 'slide'. A Germanic word. 'Slipper', C15th., is a derivative. 'Slippery' is C16th. 'Slipshod', C16th. orig. meant 'wearing slippers': 'shod' is related to 'shoe', OE., which is a Germanic word with no known cognates.

Slogan
C16th. f. OIr. 'war-cry', *sluagh* 'army' + *ghairm* 'shout'. The king's warcry in Shakeapeare's *Henry V,* 'God for Harry, England and Saint George!' is a far cry (so to speak) from modern advertising. This word has dropped a long way. But it is a good example of something written by Richard Chenevix Trench in 1855 (quoted by David Crystal and Hilary Crystal 2000): 'But while it is . . . true that words will ride very slackly at anchor on their etymologies . . . Very few have broken away and drifted from their moorings altogether.' 'War-cry' and 'advertisement' are not so far apart.

Sloth
C12th. 'Sluggishness'. The slow creature didn't acquire the word until C17th. 'Slow', OE., is a Germanic word with an obscure IE. origin.

Slug
C15th. prob. of Scand. origin.

Slum
C19th. of unknown origin.

Slut
C14th. of unknown origin.

Smile
C13th. prob. Scand.: Swed. has *smila* and Danish *smile*.

Smith
OE. A Germanic word. The preponderance of this name as a surname is due to the fact that 'smith' meant 'worker' or 'craftsman'. The farrier sense arrived later. There weren't *that* many blacksmiths.

Smithereens
C19th. The word 'smither', of unknown origin, is behind this word; perhaps f. Irish *smidirin*.

Smooch
C20th. US. origin unknown, though perhaps imit. of a kiss.

Smooth
OE. This word has no known cognates in any other IE. language.

Smug
C16th. of unknown origin.

Smuggle
C17th. of unknown origin, thought LG. has *smukkelen*, and versions of the word are in several Germanic languages.

SNAFU
C20th. Br. Army slang. An acrostic for (polite version) 'Situation Normal, All Fouled Up'.

Snail
OE. a Germanic word: ON. has *snigill*.

Snake
OE. a Germanic word: OHG. has *snahhan* 'crawl'. Irish has *snaighim* 'crawl'.

Sneeze
C15th. of imit. origin. OE. was *fnese*.

Sniff
C14th. of imit. origin.

Snigger
C18th. of imit. origin.

Snob
C18th. This word for 'cobbler' was adopted at Cambridge University to mean 'townsman'. By C19th. the word meant 'those who admired the members of the class above them', and William Thackaray (*Book of Snobs* 1848) cemented the meaning.

Snooker
C19th. of unknown origin.

Snooze
C18th. of unknown origin, prob. influenced by >sneeze and 'doze'.

Snot
C15th. a Germanic word: MD. is *snotte*.

Snow
OE. The Germanic word is there in Ger. *Schnee* and Danish *sne*. The IE. root also led to L. *nix* then Fr. *neige* and many other words (It. and Sp., to take two examples). 'Snowdrop' is C17th.

Snub
C14th. f. ON. languages, but beyond that of unknown origin.

Soap
OE. a Germanic word.

Sober
C17th. f. L. *sobrius.*

Soccer
C19th. This was derived from the middle of Association Football, the 'er' added in what was to become a typical public school way. What you call this game is socially significant. If you use this term, you are either American, or have a public school background. 'Football' is preferred elsewhere by fans: they don't care about the confusion with Rugby Union (or 'rugger' >Rugby) or Rugby League Football.

Sodomy
C13th. f. the name of the town *Sodom* (Gen. 18), and therefore the source for word. But note Ezek. 16.49–51, who lists the sins of Sodom as 'pride, fullness of bread, and . . . idleness': not homosexuality.

Sofa
C17th. f. Arab. *suffa* through Fr.

Soft
OE. a Germanic word meaning 'pleasant' or 'mild'. When Romeo, in his famous soliloquy says, 'But soft, what light from yonder window breaks?' (*Romeo and Juliet* 2:2) he is telling himself to be quiet.

Soil
C14th. f. L. *solium* 'seat', perhaps confused with *solum* 'land'; through Anglo Norman *soil* 'land'. The meaning, C13th., 'to make dirty' is, surpringly, a different word altogether, and comes ultimately f. L. *suculus* 'little pig'.

Solar
C15th. f. L. *sol* 'sun'.

Soldier
C13th. f. OFr. *soudier*, ult. f. L. *solidus* a gold coin. The underlying sense is the pay a soldier received.

Sole
C14th. To mean the part of the foot, f. L. *solum* 'bottom', 'base'. The fish, C14th., is so named because of its shape. The meaning 'single' is f. a different word, also f. L., *solus* alone.

Solemn
C14th. f. L. *sollemnis*, meaning 'celebrated at a fixed time each year'.

Solid
C14th. f. L. *solidus.*

Soliloquy
C17th. f. L. *solus* 'alone' and *loqui* 'speak'.

Solitary
C14th. F. L. *solus*. 'Solo', C17th., comes f. the same source, but (like most musical terms) it comes to us through It. Another descendant is the name of the game 'Solitaire', C18th., which before 1500 meant 'widow'.

Sombre
C18th. f. L. *sub* 'under' and *umbra* 'shade'. 'Sombrero', C16th., has the same root, having travelled through Sp. *sombre* 'shade'. 'Umbrella', C17th., is etymologically 'a little shade', having come through It. *ombrella*. The Br. climate changed the meaning. 'Umbrage', C15th., is f. the same root.

Some
OE. This word goes back to an IE. root, and is present in Gk. *hamos*, Sanskr. *sama*. It has died out in most other Germanic languages.

Somnambulist
C18th. f. L. *somnus* 'sleep' and *ambulare* 'walk'. 'Somnolent', C15th., is f. the L. too.

Son
OE. Like all the words to do with human relatives, this is very old and its cognates are nearly everywhere in the IE. family, for example: *syn*, in Russian, Polish and Czech. Eng. gets it f. the Germanic: Ger. is *Sohn*.

Song
OE. f. a Germanic root.

Soon
OE. f. a Germanic root. There's a little human nature in this word's story. It orig. meant 'immediately', but because we put things off, it is now vague, and can mean anything from 'in ten minutes' to 'next month sometime'. The same happened to 'presently'. Its original meaning can be inferred from this exchange between Ariel and Prospero: 'Presently? Ay: with a twink' (*The Tempest* 4:1).

Sophisticated
C14th. f. Gk. *sophos* 'skilled, clever'. The meaning became pejorative, however: the C5th. philosophers, the Sophists, were despised for using clever arguments to blow smoke over the truth, and that survives in Eng. 'sophistry', C14th. The modern meaning of 'sophisticated' is C20th.

Sorbet
C16th. f. Turkish *serbet* 'sherbet'; orig. Arab. *sharbat* 'drink'.

Sordid
C16th. f. L. *sordere* 'be dirty'.

Sore
OE. a Germanic word: OHG. has *ser*. It used to denote physical as well as mental pain, but now the latter meaning resides in 'sorry', a word f. the same root.

Sorrow
OE. f. a Germanic word meaning 'care', and etymologically unrelated to the above.

SOS
C20th. A folk etymology says that this is an acronym for 'save our souls' or 'save our ships', but it isn't. It is the internationally agreed Morse signal for the letters (three dots, three dashes, three dots) for the three letters, chosen because it was easy to transmit. >mayday.

Sot
OE. to mean 'fool', C16th., 'drunk'. f. MedL. *sottus*. Of unknown origin, but the word is in Sp. and Port.: *zot*.

Soul
OE. f. a Germanic root, present in Ger. for example, *Seele*. The word may be related to Gk. *ailos* 'quick-moving', with the sense of something fleeting. On the other hand, *Chambers* says that is has no cognates outside Germanic languages, and suggests a root meaning 'coming from the sea', because it was believed that the soul resided there before birth and after death.

Sound
C13th. f. L. *sonus*.

Soup
C17th. f. OFr. *soupe*, f. late L. *suppa*. The related word 'sop' meant 'piece of bread' over which the broth was poured.

Sour
A Germanic word, present in Ger. *Sauer*.

South
OE. a Germanic word. There may be a base which means 'sun', so the word may mean 'towards the region of the sun'.

Souvenir
C18th. f. L. *subvenire* 'come to the mind'.

Soy
C17th. f. Japanese *shoyu*. But the word is prob. Chinese in origin, and we get it through Du.

Spa
C17th. f. the name of a town in Belgium.

Spaghetti
C19th. It., of course: a diminutive of *strago* (of unknown origin) 'string'.

Spam
C20th. This name for a much-detested tinned meat, once celebrated in a Monty Python sketch, comes from the first and last letters of *sp*iced h*am*. Nobody liked the stuff, and it became a name for unwanted emails.

Spaniel
C14th. f. *Hispaniola* 'Spain': a Sp. dog.

Spank
C18th. of imit. origin.

Sparrow
OE. A Germanic word., though the word prob. appears in Gk. *sparasion*.

Speak
OE. A Germanic word.

Special
C13th. f. L. *specialis*, with *species*, C15th., in the background, 'look of something', then 'type'.

Speed
OE. Orig. 'success', which survives in the phrase 'Good speed'; a Germanic word. OHG. is *spuoen* 'success'.

Sperm
C14th. f. Gk. *sperma* 'seed'.

Spider
OE. a derivative of OE. *spinnan* 'spin', which came f. an early Germanic word. The origin is preserved more clearly in ModGer. *Spinne* and Du. *spinner*.

Spinach
C16th. f. OFr. *espinache*. Ult., the word was Arab., *isfinaj*, and came to Sp. via Catalan *espinac*.

Spirit
C13th. f. L. *spiritus* 'breath, life'. This word is present in many Eng. examples, such as 'aspire', C15th., 'inspire', C14th., 'expire', C15th. There are cognates in Old Slavic and Serbo-Croat.

Splendid
C17th. f. L. *splendidus* 'bright, shining'. There are cognates in few other languages; Welsh, for example, has *llathru* 'shining'. *Chambers* doubts this, and only quotes Lithuanian *splendeti* 'shine'. The word is there in Eng. 'resplendent', C15th.

Spoof
C19th. This was orig. the name of a hoaxing game. The word and the game were invented by the comedian Arthur Roberts (1852–1933).

Spoon
OE. f. Germanic and Scand. source: ON. is *sponn*, OHG. *span*.

Spoonerism
C19th. 'You have hissed my mystery lectures and tasted a whole worm and you must leave by the next town drain'. This is almost certainly an apocryphal Spoonerism, composed by mischievous students. Rev. William Spooner (1844–1930) was Warden of New College, Oxford. He reputedly transposed the initial consonants (usually) of words in his sentences: 'half-warmed fish' for 'half-formed wish', for example. The technical term for a Spoonerism is 'metathesis'.

Sporran
C19th., f. Scot Gael. and Irish Gael.: *sporan*, *sparan* respectively. f. L. *bursa* 'purse', which Eng. has in 'bursar', C13th. Though neither *Chambers* nor *Webster* gives the L. origin, *SOED* does. The word came into Eng. in Walter Scott's novel *Rob Roy* (1818).

Sport
C15th. f. AN. *desporter* 'carry away' (*des* = 'away' and *porter* 'carry'). Original meaning merely 'amusement', the modern meaning is C16th.

Sprawl
OE. unknown origin.

Spring
OE. f. 'place of rising' especially of a stream to 'season of the year', this is essentially the same Germanic word with an IE. root which signifies 'rapid movement'. It appears in Sankr. and Gk. So the season 'Spring' is 'the rising of the year'.

Spy
C13th. A Germanic word with an IE. root, it appears in OHG. *spehon*.

Squalid
C16th. f. L. *squalere* 'be dry, rough'.

Squaw
C17th. The buzz in the US is that the word is a Mohawk term for the female genitals, and is therefore offensive. This is not true. It is Algonquian for 'woman'.

Squabble
C17th. a Germanic word with an IE. root. There is a dialect Swed. word *skvabbel*.

Squawk
C19th. of imit. origin, as are 'squeak', C14th. and 'squeal', C13th.

Squeeze
C16th. of origin unknown.

Squelch
C17th. a Germanic word, presumably imit.

Squiffy
C19th. of unknown origin.

Squirrel
C14th. f. L. *sciurus* and Gk. *skiouros*.

Stag
C12th. of obscure origin, though ON. has *staggr* 'male bird'.

Stalactite
C17th., and Stalagmite, C18th. The first is f. Gk. *stalaktos* 'dripping', the second f. *stalagmos* 'a dropping'.

Stanza
C16th. f. It. 'stopping place'. f. L. *stare* 'stand'. This word is the correct one for what is a 'verse' in a song.

Star
OE. It is everywhere in the family of IE. languages. Some examples: *atar* (Sansk.), *astr* (Gk.), *stella* (L). Fr. *etoile* may not sound like the other words, but it is related. So are the Ger. *Stern* (we get the word f. a Germanic source), It. *stella*, Sp. *estrella* and Swed. *stjarna*.

Statue
C14th. f. L. *statua*, after *stare* 'stand'.

Steak
C15th. f. ON. *steik*, related to *steikja* 'roast'.

Steep
OE. f. a prehistoric Germanic base. f. which came 'Steeple', also OE. A 'steeplechase', C18th., was so-named because the original races were run with church steeples marking the finishing lines.

Stew

This word meant 'brothel', C14th., centuries before it arrived at its commoner meaning, C18th. Indeed, the brothel meaning was secondary, because it orig. meant 'steam bath'; but like the Roman baths in Martial's C1st. poems, the early English ones seemed to have had more than one function. The word is a descendant, through L., of Gk. *tuphos* 'steam'. OFr. is *estuve*.

Stilton

C18th. Named after an inn in a Cambridgeshire village, where the cheese was orig. sold (not made).

Sting

OE. f. ON. *stanga* 'pierce'. It has a Germanic root. The sense of an 'ill-tempered or niggardly person' is reflected in 'stingy', C17th.

Stink

OE. a Germanic word. It meant 'smell' at first; 'smell bad' emerged later. 'Reek', OE., was also neutral in Shakespeare's time: he is not being offensive when he writes in Sonnet 130 about 'the breath that from my mistress reeks'.

Stomach

C14th. f. Gk. *stomakhos*, f. *stoma* 'mouth'.

Storm

OE. a Germanic word: OHG. is *sturm*, ON. is *stormr*. Like many sea-associated words, for example, 'sail', 'oar', 'mast', this came with the Vikings. As Hitchings says, you can almost hear the roaring and the hissing of the sea in many of them.

Story

C13th. f. L. *historia*, through OFr. *estoire*.

Strange

C13th. The OFr. is *estrange*. f. L. *extraneus*.

Strangle

C13th. f. Gk. *straggalan* through L. *strangulare*. The Gk. stems f. *straggale* 'halter'.

Straw

OE. a Germanic word: OHG. is *stro*. The origin of 'Strawberry', also OE., is obscure.

Stream

OE. A Germanic word – OHG. is *stroum* – with an IE. Root which is behind Gk. *rhreuma*. OIr. is *sruaim*.

Street
OE. a Germanic word: OHG. is *strazza*, Ger. is *Strasse*, and outside Germanic, late L. is *strata*.

Strumpet
C14th. Of unc. orig., but one tentative suggestion is L. *stuprare* 'have illicit sex with'.

Stud
OE. a Germanic word – OHG. is *stuot*. The sense 'sexually active male' is C19th.

Student
C15th. f. L. *studere* 'be eager'. 'Study' is C13th., 'metal effort'; to mean 'place to work mentally', C14th., f. L. *studium* 'painstaking application'.

Stupid
C16th. f. L. *stupere* 'be stunned'. There is an IE. root which led to Gk. *tuptein* 'hit'.

Style
C13th. f. L. *stilus*. The letter 'y' is there because the word was wrongly thought to be Gk.

Sub-
This L. prefix denotes 'under'. A few examples: 'subdue', C14th., *ducere* 'bring'; 'subject', C14th., *jacere* 'throw'; 'subscribe', C15th. *scribere* 'write'. 'Subway', C19th., is a modern example. In 'suffocate', the 'b' has been lost; *fauces* 'throat'.

Sudden
C13th. f. L. *subito*.

Sufi
C17th. This Muslim sect is named after Arab. *sufi* 'wool'.

Sugar
C13th. Orig. f. Arab. *sukkar*, then through MedL. *succarum*.

Sultan
C16th., Arab. for 'power, dominion'. *Sultana*, also C16th. is the feminine version. C19th., the fem. version was applied to a raisin.

Summer
OE. a Germanic word – OHG. is *sumar* – with an IE. base which appears in both Irish and Welsh: *sam*, *ham*.

Sun
OE. f. an IE. root which has developed in Germanic languages (including Eng.) giving, for example, German *Sonne*; and in slightly different ways in Rom. languages, *via* L. *sol*; for example, Fr. *soleil*.

Sunni
C17th. A Muslim who accepts tradition as having authority as well as The >Qur'an. f. *sunna* 'tradition'.

Super
f. L. word meaning 'above'. So 'superior', C14th., 'situated above'. 'Superstructure', C20th., is a modern example. 'Superman', C20th., is a translation by George Bernard Shaw of Ger. *Ubermensch*. ('mensch' = 'human being').

Supercalifragilisticexpialidocious
C20th. Was the invention of the lyricists Robert B and Richard M Sherman for the musical *Mary Poppins* based on the novels by Mary Travers. It is here so that I can repeat the best pun of all. Some years ago, the minnow Scottish football team Inverness Caledonian Thistle (Cally for short) beat mighty Celtic 3–1. The headline over the report in *The Sun* read SUPER CALLY GO BALLISTIC, CELTIC ARE ATROCIOUS.

Sure
f. L. *securus*.

Sushi
C19th. This word for a dish of cold cooked rice and raw fish is, of course, Japanese.

Swallow
OE. For the bird's name: a Germanic word (Ger. *Schwalbe*). The word meaning 'ingest' is also OE., and also Germanic (Ger. *Schwelgen*).

Swan
OE. a Germanic word (Ger. *Swann*). It may have come f. an IE. base meaning 'sound', which L. has in *sonare*.

Swastika
C19th. f. Sanskr. *svasti* 'well-being'. The first Nazi use of the word was in 1932.

Swear
OE. a Germanic word: Ger. is *Schworen*.

Sweat
OE. A word that goes back to IE., and which is widespread in all branches of the family: Gk. *hidros*, L. *sudor* and many Germanic words including this one. 'Sweater', the wollen garment, arrived in C19th., and denoted a garment worn to produce sweat and so reduce weight.

Sweet
OE. Another word that goes back to IE., and which is widespread in all branches of the family: Gk. *hedus*, for example, f. which we get 'hedonism' and L. *suavis*, f. which get 'suave'. A derivative is 'sweetheart',

C13th., which is not rhyming slang for, nor a shortening of, 'tart', but simply the term of endearment it sounds.

Swift
OE. The base is *swifan* 'move on a course'; related to ON. *svifa*. It was C17th. before the word was use for the bird.

Swig
C16th. of unknown origin.

Swindle
C18th. f. Ger. *Schwindler* 'cheat'; the word goes back to older Germanic roots.

Sym-, syn-
These Gk. prefixes denote 'together', 'alike' etc. So: 'symmetry', C16th. (*metron*, 'measure'); 'sympathy', C16th., (*pathos* 'feeling'); 'symphony', C13th. (*phone* 'sound'). A 'symposium', C18th., was a drinking party (*potes* 'drinker' which, of course, we have in 'potion', C13th).

Synagogue
C12th. f. Gk. meaning 'meeting', f. *syn-* + *agein* 'lead'; then late L. *synagoga*. The meaning 'Jewish assembly place' arose because the translators of the Bible wrote in Gk. The equivalent Heb. Word is *knesset*, now used for the name of the Israeli parliament.

T

Tabasco
C17th. f. the name of a river (and state) in Mexico.

Tabby
C17th. to mean 'striped taffeta'. f. Arab. *Al-attabiya*, part of Baghdad where the stuff was made. By C18th., it was used for a striped cat.

Table
C12th., f. L. *tabula* 'plank'.

Taboo
C18th. f. Tongan *tabu*. This one of the words brought back by the explorer James Cook (1728–1779).

Tadpole
C15th. A ME. word which combines *tadde* >toad and *pol* 'head'.

Talk
C13th. A word that has only one relative, Old Frisian *talken*. This language was spoken in northern parts of what is now the Netherlands and Germany, especially on the islands. English-speaking visitors have told me that it is possible to understand, with a little attention, local speech. This word is a relic of that link. It has Germanic roots, but nothing else has survived.

Tandoor
C20th. Urdu 'oven'.

Tangerine
C19th. f. *Tangier* whence the fruit came.

Tango
C20th. f. Amer. Sp.

Tank
C17th. f. Guj. *taku* 'reservoir'. C20th., the word was used for 'armoured vehicle' in the interests of secrecy.

Tankard
C14th. of unknown origin, though MD. has *tanckaert*.

Tantrum
C18th. of unknown origin.

Tar
OE. f. a Germanic root, prob. f. a word for 'tree': some trees produce a thick black liquid. 'Tarpaulin', C17th., is *tar* + 'pall', OE., being a thick cloth, f. L. *pallium* 'cloak'. 'Tarpaulin', C17th., is also a nickname for a sailor, now always shortened to 'tar'. 'Tarmac', C19th., is a trademark.

Taste
C13th. Orig. this meant to test something by touching it, but had its current meaning by C16th. f. L. *tangere* 'touch' mixed with *gustare* 'taste'.

Tattoo
There are two unrelated words: first, the military use (drumroll, display of military skills), C18th., comes f. Du. *taptoe*, a signal for closing time: 'shut the [beer] taps'; used in Eng. as signal, 'back to barracks'; the second word, for 'bodily decoration' (if that is the *mot juste*) is also C18th., and of Polynesian origin, prob. Tahitian. In James Cook's journals, it is *tattow*.

Tawdry
C17th. As the great Johnson defines it, 'splendid without cost . . . the kind of necklace worn by country wenches'. It was sold at St Audrey's fair; f. whence the word. She (proper name Etheldrida) is the patron saint of Ely.

Tax
C13th. f. L. *taxare*.

Tea
C17th. f. Mandarin dialect *ch'a*, whence also comes the informal word 'char'.

Teach
OE. ult. f. an IE. word for 'show', which led to a Gk. word and to Germanic words with the same meaning, f. whence it arrived in Eng.

Technical
C17th. f. Gk. *tekhne* 'art'.

Teddy bear
C20th. f. the pet name of Theodore Roosevelt (US. president 1901–1909), who hunted bears.

Teetotal
C19th. the 'tee' was added to 'total' to emphasise that beer was excluded as well as the hard stuff, whisky and the like. Or perhaps the passionate anti-drinking speaker had a stammer.

Tele-
This Gk. prefix denotes 'afar'. Some examples are: 'telephone', C19th., 'far-speaker'. A classically educated character in Kingsley Amis's novel *A Girl Like You* facetiously calls it that. 'Telescope', C17th., is a 'far-see-er'. 'Television', C20th., would probably have been called 'far-see-er' were it not for the dominance of the classics in public schools in Victorian and early C20th. times. The second part of the word is f. L. *visio* (not Gk.) 'I see', and the hybrid nature of this derivation used to irritate a schoolmaster in a grammar school in the early 1960s.

Temper
C14th. f. L. *temperare* 'restrain oneself, blend'. Our usage in, for example, 'I'll temper that remark with the opposite point of view' is closer to its etymology than its customary modern meaning.

Temple
There are two unrelated words: the first is OE., f. L. *templum* 'consecrated space'; the second, C14th., is f. L. *tempus* 'time', and it may refer obscurely to time through the concept of 'span', here a span of skin.

Tennis
Possibly f. OFr. *tenez* 'hold', the server's cry to his opponent. But this sounds like an early folk mythology; origin unknown.

Terrestrial
C15th. f. L. *terra* >earth, as is the name of the Medi*terra*nean Sea (the middle of the world to the Romans, and that is the primary meaning, not that the sea is in the middle of land, even though it is). 'Territory', C15th., and 'terrestrial', also C15th., are f. the same source.

Terror
C14th. f. L. *terror*.

Testicle
C15th. f. L. *testis*. This gland bears witness, like a third party (the word goes back to an IE. word *tris* meaning 'three') to a man's virility. Hence 'testament' and 'testimony', both C14th.

Text
C14th. f. L. *textus* 'tissue', f. a verb *texere* 'weave', a metaphor for the act of writing. 'Textile', C17th., and 'texture' , C17th., are f. the same source, but without the metaphorical sense.

Thank
OE. a Germanic word: Ger. has *Danken*.

Theatre
C14th. f. Gk. *theatron* 'place for viewing'.

Theft
OE. A Germanic word with a cognate in (among others) Old Frisian, considered by many authorities to be a very close relation to Eng.: *thiufte*.

Theism
C17th. f. Gk. *theos* 'god'. 'Theology', C14th., is 'the study of God'. >logy 'Atheism', C16th., is f. the negative *a* + *theos*.

Theory
C16th. f. Gk. *theoria*, f. *theoros* 'spectator', and related to >theatre.

Thesaurus
C19th. f. Gk. for 'treasure', through L.

Thin
OE. a Germanic word with an IE. root also represented in L. *tenuis*, f. which we get 'attenuate' and 'tenuous'.

Thing
OE. 'Assembly', and this meaning is there is a ghostly way in our 'hustings', and more clearly in the name of the Icelandic parliament, *Althing*. The root notion is 'time': hustings happen at an appointed time. The word came to mean 'something discussed at a gathering', and then, by C16th., an entity.

Think
OE. a Germanic word: Ger. and Du. are *denken*.

Thirst
OE. The IE. root led to L. *torrere* 'dry', present in (among other languages) Irish *tart*.

Thousand
OE. a Germanic word with a cousin in Lithuanian, which Barford says is probably the closest to IE.: *tukstantis*.

Thrift
C13th. This word is related to 'thrive', and it orig. meant 'thriving condition'. It's f. an ON. word

Throat
OE. a Germanic word.

Throne
C13th. f. Gk. *thronos*.

Throw
OE. a Germanic word with an IE. root seen in L. *terere* 'rub'.

Thug
C19th. f. Hindi *thag* 'cheat', 'robber'.

Thumb
OE. a Germanic word f. an IE. word denoting 'swelling'.

Thunder
OE. An IE. root meaning 'sound' has led to this Germanic word, to the Eng. word, and, by a different route, to L. *tonare*.

Tiddly, tiddlywink
C19th. These words are of unknown origin but it has been suggested that they come f. Cockney rhyming slang for 'drink'. Why the game is called that is even more obscure. For some time the second word was slang for 'public house'.

Tide
OE. to mean 'period': for example, 'Christmastide', 'eventide'; by C14th. it meant 'sea's movement'; f. a Germanic word with an IE. root meaning 'divide', also present in Gk. and Sanskr. High tide and low tide happen at fixed times. 'Tidy' is f. the same source, and orig. meant 'timely', acquiring its present meaning in the C13th.

Tie
OE. a Germanic word.

Tiger
C13th. f. Gk. and L. *tigris*.

Time
OE. f. the same IE. base as >tide.

Tin
OE. a Germanic word of obscure origin.

Tiny
C16th. origin obscure. It was originally paired with 'little', as in, 'When that I was a little tiny boy', the song that ends Shakespeare's *Twelfth Night*.

Titanic
C17th. f. the name of a race of giants in Gk. mythology; now inextricably linked to the fate of the tragic ship.

Titbit
C17th. Perhaps 'tid' was a dialect word that meant 'nice'. I am told that the old spelling, with the 'd', is used in US, as the Eng. spelling is considered vulgar, much as Americans say 'white meat' for 'breast' when handing round turkey on Thanksgiving Day. But it's also possible that

US. Eng. has simply kept the Elizabethan spelling, much as it has kept Elizabethan usage in, for example, 'gotten'.

Toad
OE. a mystery word, with no relatives in any other language.

Tobacco
C16th. f. Sp. and Port. *tabaco*, of unc. orig. The traditional suggestion is that it comes f. the Caribbean, and was brought back by Iberian explorers, and both *Webster* and *SOED* give this etymology. But another suggestion is that, because It. had *tabacco* and Sp. *tabaco* in C15th. (before the discovery of the New World), the word was used for various medicinal herbs. Thus, it comes f. Arab. *tabbaq*. It is possible that the Sp. adopted the old word for the new plant.

Toe
OE. a Germanic word of unknown origin.

Toerag
C19th. f. the name of the sacking that workers in the grainhouses of the London docks wore over their boots. But it was probably used for any poor person, such as a tramp, who protected his or her feet with rags.

Toffee
C19th. orig. *taffy*, and sometimes spelt *toughy*, this is a mystery word. The notion that the last spelling suggests that the names come f. the chewiness of the revolting tooth-rotting stuff sounds like a folk etymology.

Toilet
C16th. f. Fr. *toilette*, 'little cloth'. Later, a word for a lady's dressing table, and the act of dressing itself. Its normal usage is probably the most common euphemism in the language, and sounds to many modern ears genteel. The search for a non-euphemistic word goes on, except among the irredeemably coarse. Americans are offended by it, despite its impeccably polite origin; hence their 'restroom', 'bathroom', 'comfort station' etc. When I was a teenager, a girlfriend's mother suggested that her daughter might show me 'the geography of the house'. >lavatory for another euphemism.

A digression on euphemisms for this word: In the *Authorised Version of the Bible*, Judg. 3.24 says that the unfortunate king Eglon was assassinated as he 'covered his feet'. Other Br. translations give 'was relieving himself'. The *Bible in Basic English* says that he was occupied in 'a private purpose' (how basic is that English?). The *Douay-Rheims Bible* says that he was 'easing nature'. No modern translation that I have come across has given this word as 'in the jakes' or 'john', or 'crapping', or even 'emptying his bladder/bowels'.

Tomato

C17th. f. Sp. and Port. *tomate*; f. *Nahuatl*. The Eng. spelling was prob. influenced by 'potato'.

Tomb

C13th. f. Gk. *tombos* 'mound'.

Tongue

OE., both for the muscle in the mouth and for 'language'. A Germanic word with an IE. root which also produced L. *lingua*. Welsh *tafod* come f. the same source.

Tooth

OE. This is a very old word, and its source is represented in all three main branches of the IE. family; L., for example, is *dens*, f. which we get 'dental'. Eng. gets it f. a Germanic source.

Tor

OE. a rare thing: a word f. Celt. Old Welsh. is *twrr* 'bulge'.

Tornado

C16th. f. Sp. *tronada*, f. *tronar* 'thunder'; later assimilated to *tonar* 'turn'.

Tortoise

C15th. f. Fr. *tortue*, of unknown origin.

Tory

C16th. This orig. meant 'robber'. f. Irish *toraighe* 'pursuer'. It came to be used as a term of abuse for Catholic Royalists, and for supporters of the Catholic Duke of York, later James II, in his succession to the throne. The connection with the political party is not, of course, that its members are 'robbers' – good heavens no – but that the party had orig. opposed the removal of James. The name, which was applied by opponents pejoratively, implying something like 'wild Irishmen leading the country to the Church of Rome' was changed to 'Conservative' in 1830, but, for some reason, it sticks.

Total

C14th. f. L. *totalis*.

Totem

C18th. an Algonquian word.

Traffic

C16th. f. Fr. *traffique*. It goes back to It., but beyond there, nothing is known.

Tragedy
C14th. f. Gk. *tragos* 'goat' + *oide* 'song'. This surprising etymology stems, possibly, from costumes worn in performances in ancient Greece; or perhaps from a prize awarded for the best performance.

Traitor
C13th. f. L. >*trans* + *dare* 'give'. The powerful image is of someone being handed over to the other side. 'Treason', C13th., has the same derivation.

Tramp
C14th., prob. Du.; MLG. is *trampen*.

Tranquil
C17th. f. L. *tranquillus*.

Trans-
This L. prefix denotes 'across', beyond', 'over'. A few examples: 'transfer', C14th. (*ferre* 'bear'); 'transexual', C20th.; 'transport', C14th., (*portare* 'carry').

Treachery
C13th. f. OFr. *trecherie* 'cheat'. The word is not connected to >traitor or >treason, which both derive f. L.

Treason
>traitor

Treasure
C12th. f. L. *thesaurus*.

Tree
OE. A word widely present, as one might expect, in Germanic languages, it goes back to an IE. root which is also present in Gk. *doru* and Sanskr. *daru*. Welsh *derwen* is 'oak', and OIr. is *daur*. >tree.

Trek
C19th. a South African word f. MD. *trekken* 'pull'. >trigger.

Trespass
C13th. f. MedL. *transpassare*; >*trans* + *passare* ('pass across').

Tri-
This L. and Gk. prefix denotes 'three'. A few examples: 'triangle', C14th. (*angelus* L. 'angle'); 'tricolour', C18th. (L. *color*); 'tricycle', C19th. (Gk. *kuklos* 'circle').

Trifle
C13th., 'idle talk'. C14th., 'knick-knack'; C16th., finally the pudding meaning emerges. f. Fr. *truffe* 'deceit'.

Trigger
C17th. f. Du. *trekken* 'pull', related to >trek.

Troll
There are two unrelated words in Eng. C14th., to mean 'saunter' is of unknown origin, but Fr. has *troller* 'wander casually'. In the middle C20th., the word acquired a particular homosexual meaning, 'cruise looking for a pick-up', with which much fun was had in two mid-C20th. Br. radio shows, *Round the Horn* and *Beyond our Ken*. The word 'trolley', C19th., is related to the word, without the gay implications.

The other word, C19th., denotes 'dwarf', 'hobgoblin' etc. and is f. Scand. mythology. f. ON., f. whence it arrived in Sc.

Trollop
C17th. of origin unknown.

Trombone
>trumpet

Trouble
C13th., 'mental distress'; C14th., 'disturbance'. f. L. *turbidus*.

Trousers
C17th. This is an extension (under the influence of 'drawers') of *trouse* (C16th). f. the Sc. Gaelic *triubhas* and Irish *trius*.

Trout
OE. f. late L. *tructa*.

True
OE. A widespread Germanic word, also in Sanskr. *dhruvas*, which also produced our 'truce'. Possibly related in ancient times to words for 'oak' (>tree): the Sanskr. means 'hard, firm'.

Trumpet
C13th. OFr. *trompe*, whence also 'trombone', C18th.

Trust
C13th. Obscure, but with relatives in most Germanic languages. Possibly f. the same base as >truth.

Try
C13th. orig 'sift', as is visible in OFr. *trier* 'pick out', which in turn comes f. an unknown Rom. word.

Tsunami
C20th. f. Japanese *tsu* 'harbour' + *nami* 'wave'.

Tulip
C17th. ult. f. a Pers. word, whence it went into Turkish as *tuliband*, which means 'turban', C16th. The flower got its name because of the perceived resemblance.

Turd
OE. This, unsurprisingly, is an ancient and widespread word with an IE. root denoting 'separation' (>shit). Eng. gets the word f. an old Germanic root.

Turkey
C16th. The African guinea fowl was brought into Europe through Turkey, and the Amer. turkey was perceived as resembling it.

Turnip
C16th. f. L. *napus* 'turnip'. An OE. version of the L. word survives in the Sc. 'neep' ('swede' as well as 'turnip') which are, with haggis and whisky, necessary ingredients for Burns Night suppers. The first part of the word may come f. the notion of turning, because of the vegetable's shape.

Turquoise
C14th. OFr., short for *pierre turquoise* 'Turkish stone'.

Turtle
C17th. f. Fr. *tortue*, which is of obscure origin.

Tuxedo
C19th. US., f. the name of a fashionable club, Tuxedo Park, near New York.

Tycoon
C19th. This title was given by foreigners to the >shogun of Japan, and is f. Japanese *taikun* 'great lord or prince'; f. Chinese *tai* 'great' and *kiun* 'lord'.

Tyrannosaurus
C20th. Gk. for 'tyrant lizard'.

U

Udder

OE. Versions of this word are present in nearly all IE. languages: L. has *uber.* Eng. gets it through the Germanic root.

Ugly

C13th. f. ON. *uggligr* 'to be feared'.

Ukulele

C20th. Hawaiian for 'jumping flea'. They heard the Portuguese playing their little guitars, and were not, apparently, impressed.

Umbrage

>sombre

Umbrella

>sombre

Umpire

C15th. f. OFr. *nounpere,* f. *non+peer,* 'impartial judge'. The 'n' has moved to the indefinite article in Eng., as with >adder (orig. *nadder*) and others.

Un-

This OE. prefix expresses reversal or deprivation. A few examples with obvious meanings: 'unable', C14th. (L. *habere* 'hold'); 'undo', OE.; 'undress', C17th.

Uncle

C13th. f. L. *avunculus* (f. which, of course, Eng. gets 'avuncular'). The word came to Eng. through Fr. *oncle.*

Understand

OE. In Peter Ackroyd's novel *The Lambs of London* William Ireland, who is based on a historical character, tells Mary Lamb that the word derives from the people in the pit at the Globe theatre. They 'understood' because they 'stood under'. But he was a forger. Is this how some folk etymologies begin? The word is much older than that, and come to us f. Germanic (MLG. is *understan*). Nevertheless, to 'stand under' something is to be close to it.

Unicorn
C13th. f. L. *uni* 'one' and *cornu* 'horn'.

Unique
C17th. f. L. *unus* 'one'.

Unison
C16th. f. L. *unus* 'one' + *sonus* 'sound'.

Universe
C14th. f. *unus* 'one' + *vertere* 'turn'. The name of a 'university', C14th., with the same derivation, suggests that the institution denotes the 'whole' number of people belonging to it. They are 'all one'.

Urchin
C13th. f. L. *ericius* 'hedgehog', the OE meaning. Three centuries later, it denoted 'deformed person': in Shakespeare's play *Richard III* the Duke of Gloucester, later the king (in the play, if not in life, a hunchback), is given this epithet among many others by his enemies. The modern meaning is C16th.

Usual
C14th. f. L. *usus* 'use'.

Uterus
C17th. f. L. for 'belly' or 'womb'. There is an IE. root which produced words in Sanskr. and other languages.

Uxorious
C16th. f. L. *uxor* 'wife'. This denotes what must be one of the most forgiveable of faults.

V

Vagabond
C15th. f. L. *vagari* 'wander'. 'Vagrant', C15th. and 'vague', C16th., are f. the same root.

Vagina
C17th. f. L. 'sheath'. >vanilla.

Vain
C13th. f. L. *vanus* 'empty'. The modern meaning did not emerge till C17th. 'Vanity', also C13th., comes f. the same root. When the preacher in Ecclesiastes, in the AV. of the Bible (12.8) wrote that everything was 'vanity', he meant, as modern translations tell us, 'emptiness'.

Vamp
C20th., for a woman who uses her allure to do mischief, is a shortening of . . .

Vampire
C18th. f. a word in a Russian language, *upyr* 'witch'. It found its way into Hungarian (a non-IE. language) and then to Fr. as *vampire*. There are many equivalents in Slavic. languages: Serbian *vampir*, for example. The meaning 'blood-sucking bat' is secondary and recent: C19th.

Van
C19th. a shortening of >caravan.

Vandal
C17th. f. the L. version of the name of the Wandal tribe that sacked Rome in the C5th.

Vanilla
C17th. f. L. 'sheath', presumably f. the shape of the plant. >vagina.

Vanity
>vain

Vaseline
C19th. f. Ger. *Wasser* 'water' + Gk. *elaion* 'oil'.

Veal
C14th. f. L. *vitulus* 'calf'.

Vegetable
C14th. f. L. *vegetus* 'living, active'.

Vendetta
C19th. It. 'blood-feud', f. L. *vindicta* 'vengeance'.

Venereal
C15th. f. L. *venus* 'love'. How sad it is that the word hardly exists now except in tandem with 'disease', a usage f. C17th.

Venison
C13th. to mean 'flesh of hunted animals'. It didn't mean 'deer-meat' specifically until C18th. f. L. *venari* 'hunt' >deer.

Ventriloquy
C16th. f. L. *venter* 'belly' + *loqui* 'speak'.

Verb
>word

Verse
OE. f. L. *vertere* 'turn'. *Versus* was a turn of the plough, and this is a metaphor for the beginning of each new verse, or >stanza in a >poem, in the Bible.

Very
C13th. f. L. *verus* 'true', with an IE. root. Eng. has the root in 'verify'. By C15th., the current use had emerged, and is now little more than a (usually redundant) intensifier.

Vest
C17th. f. L. *vestis* 'clothing' with an IE. root. The word has been versatile, covering clothing generally, religious clothes ('vestment'), loose outgarments for both men and women, and in the US is still used for 'waistcoat'. By C19th., it had its current Br. meaning.

Vice
There are three unrelated words: C13th., to mean 'sin', is f. L. *vitium* 'fault'; the screwed tool, C15th., is f. L. *vitis* 'wine stem'; the third, C15th., is a L. prefix meaning 'deputy', for example, 'vice-chancellor'. 'Vicar', C13th., comes f. this root. 'Viceroy', C16th., comes f. this root through Fr., *roi* meaning 'king'.

Viking
C19th. There are two theories about this word. The traditional one is that it comes f. ON. *vikingr*, f. *vik* 'inlet, fjord'. But the word has been

found in OE., C8th., which suggests that it comes f. Old Frisian *wik* 'camp'. Note that the word was not used in Eng. until it became a historian's term in C19th.

Vile

C13th. f. L. *vilis* 'of low value', and not related to . . .

Villain

C14th. f. L. *villa* 'country house'. The man lived as a serf in the *villa*'s grounds. 'Village' comes f. the same root.

Vine

>wine

Vinegar

C13th. f. L. *vinum* 'wine' + *acer* 'sour'.

Viola, violin

C18th., C16th., both f. It. *viola.* There is a L. root, which is the name of the goddess of joy, *Vitula.* They are nothing to do with 'violet', C14th., which is f. an IE. root which led to Gk. *ion*, present in Eng. 'iodine', and L. *viola* 'violet'.

Viper

C16th. f. L. *vipera*, 'snake'. It comes f. two earlier words, *vivus* 'alive', and *parere* 'give birth'. It was believed that the snake gave birth to live offspring. f. the former Eng. gets 'vivid', and f. the latter 'parent'.

Virago

OE. The Vulgate (L.) translation of Genesis, AD 405, gives Gen. 2.23 as: *Haec vocabitur virago, quonoiam de viro sumpta est*: 'she shall be called Woman, because she was taken out of man'. The third word has stuck to mean 'man-like woman', and is worn with pride by some feminists, for example, the publisher Virago, which only produces books by women. *Vir* is L. man.

Virgin

C13th. f. L. *virgo.*

Virile

C15th. f. L. *vir* 'man'. There are words descending f. the same IE. root in Germanic, and in Welsh and OIr. *gwr* and *fer.*

Virginals

C16th. prob. named because the plucked keyboard instrument was suitable for playing by young women.

Vision
C13th. f. L. *videre* 'see'.

Visit
C13th. f. L. *visitare*.

Vodka
C19th. A Russian diminutive of *voda* 'water'. >whisk[e]y'.

Volcano
C17th. f. the name of the Roman god of fire, *Vulcanus*.

Voodoo
C19th. f. Dahomey *vodu*.

Voyage
C13th. f. L. *viaticum* 'provisions for a journey'; then 'journey' itself.

Voyeur
C20th. f. Fr. *voir* 'see', ult. f. L. *videre*.

Vulgar
C14th. f. L. *volgus* 'the common people'.

W

Wagon

C16th. f. Du. *wagen* and *waghen*, which is visible in the title of Constable's famous picture, *The Hay Wain*, f. a Germanic root.

Wagtail

C16th. a simple, obvious and charming derivation.

Waist

C14th. a Germanic word.

Wait

C12th., 'watch as a spy', as in the phrase 'lie in wait'; C14th., 'await'; C16th. 'serve food'. f. Old Northern Fr. *waitier*; with a Germanic root.

Wake

OE. a Germanic word.

Walk

OE. a Germanic word of unknown origin that orig. meant 'roll about', and which only took on its present meaning in C13th.

Wall

OE. f. L. *vallum* 'rampart'.

Walnut

OE. The word's etymology tells us that it stands for a foreign nut. But who called it that, and who were the foreigners? *Collins* says the word comes f. OE. *walh-hnutu*, and that the tree was Asian and not imported in Britain till C15th. So the Asians were the foreigners. *Chambers*, on the other hand, says that the foreigners were the southern Celt. neighbours of Germanic peoples: it was their tree, and not the Germanic hazel. Indeed, the first element in the word comes f. *wealh* 'foreigner', which we can see in our word >Welsh.

Walrus

C17th. a Du. word, but ON. has *hrosshvalr* 'horse-whale'. The connection between these two sources is obscure.

Waltz
C18th. f. German. *walzten* 'roll'.

Wander
OE. a Germanic word.

Wangle
C19th. This word was orig. printer's slang meaning 'to arrange something to ones own satisfaction', and is of unknown origin.

Want
C13th. f. ON. for a word denoting 'something missing'.

War
C12th. a Germanic word, just about visible today in Fr. *guerre*. OHG. *werra* = 'confusion', as does ModGer. *Wirr*. Warrior, C13th., is f. the same root. Sp. *guerilla* gave us a word for what is etymologically a 'little war'.

Wardrobe
C14th. f. OFr. *guarderobe*, f. *garder* 'keep' + 'robe'. The latter word now denotes a 'privy' in a medieval castle.

Warm
OE. a Germanic word present in the same form in ModGer. But it has an IE. root, present in L. *fornus* 'oven' (hence Modern It. *forno*, on many a menu, and Gk. *thermos*, f. whence of course the comforting flask's tradename).

Wash
OE. ult. f. a *Germanic* word for water.

Wasp
OE. This word comes to us through the Germanic languages, but, having an IE. root, it's present in other branches of the family, including L. *vespa*, after which those motor scooters swarming round Naples are named.

Water
OE. As one might expect, an ancient word. The prehistoric IE. root is *wodor*. It's there, in varying forms, in L. *unda*, 'wave', Sanskr. *udan*, Ger. *Wasser*. It's also there in Russian >*vodka* and Gael. >*whisk[e]y*. Water in It. is *acqua*, f. L. *aqua*, which we retain in many words, for example, 'aquamarine', 'aquatic' and 'aqua-lung'.

Watt
C19th. after the name of James Watt (1736–1819), a pioneer in the study of energy.

Way
OE. a Germanic word which goes back to an IE. root which also led to L. *vehere* 'carry'.

Weapon
OE. A Germanic word present in Du. *wapen*, but of unknown origin.

Weary
OE. A Germanic word whose other relatives have died out.

Weather
OE. The IE. root meant 'blow', and developed into Ger. *Wetter*, Du. *were* as well as this word.

Web
OE. a Germanic word which also produced our 'weave'.

Wed
OE. This word goes back to a Germanic root meaning 'pledge, promise', and is widespread in the old Germanic languages.

Weep
OE. f. a Germanic word with no cognates which may have developed in imitation of the sound.

Weird
OE. f. a Germanic root. orig. 'destiny', and then developed into the meaning 'fate-controlling', and Shakespeare's use of the phrase 'weird sisters' in *Macbeth* is one of the earliest usages of the word in this sense. The word has degenerated to mean 'coincidental', as in: 'I was thinking of you when you rang!' 'How weird!'

Welcome
C12th. This word comes, simply as you like, f. 'well' and 'come', and is an anglicization of OFr. *bienvenu* or ON. *velkominn*.

Wellington
C19th. f. the name of the Duke of Wellington (1769–1852). >Cardigan, >Nicotine, >Quisling, >Sandwich and for other eponymous derivations.

Welsh
OE. ult. f. L. *Volcae*, a Celt. tribe in southern Gaul, and thus foreign to the Romans. The word drifted into Germanic *walsch*, and came to mean 'non-Germanic foreigner'. The name survives in 'Welsh', as well as in the last part of 'Cornwall', and in >walnut. You can see it, too, it *Walloon*, the name of a people inhabiting southern Belgium.

Werewolf
OE. Germanic, prob. f. L. *vir* 'man' + 'wolf'.

West

OE. a Germanic word. The IE. root led to L. *vespers* (which we have to mean 'evening prayer') and Gk. *hesperos* 'evening'.

Whale

OE. a Germanic word: ModGer. is *Wal.*

Wheat

>white

Whipper-snapper

C17th. prob. f. 'whip-snapper'.

Whisky, whiskey

C18th. These words (the former Sc., the latter Irish, and later US) come f. Sc. and Irish, *usquebaugh, uisge* 'water', and *beatha* 'life'. The word is a calque of L. *aqua vita* 'water of life', an optimistic view of the stuff, we might think today. >Vodka, where the Russians don't seem to have needed the 'life' bit to justify the thing's existence. The Scand. *akvavit* has the same root, and *aqua* is visible.

Whisper

OE. an old and widespread word (e.g. ON. *hviskra*) of imit. origin.

White

OE. 'hwit'; widespread in Germanic languages, this word goes back to an IE. root which is present in Sanskr. denoting 'brightness'. 'Wheat', also OE., is f. the same source, and means 'white grain'.

Whore

OE. f. an IE. root. The Germanic stem of this word leads to German *hore* and many other words of a similar kind, including, of course, the English word. The stem that leads south, on the other hand, produces L. *carus* 'dear', which is the source of 'charity'. >Dedicatory Poem 'For Cariad'.

Wicked

C13th. a dialect word f. OE *wicca* 'wizard'. For children, this word can mean 'excellent' in a contrary development. Some children even say >sick as an exclamation of approval.

Wife

OE. This orig. meant 'woman', a usage that survives in 'old wives' tale'; a widespread Germanic word of unknown origin which Ger. no longer has (cf. their *frau*).

Wimp

C20th. prob. short for 'whimper'.

Wind

OE. a Germanic word that has a root in IE. which also produced L. *ventus*, which we have in 'ventilate'.

Window

C13th. f. ON. *vindauga, vindr* 'wind' + *auga* 'eye'. MedL. *fenester* fought with this word till C16th. >defenestrate.

Wine

OE. f. L. *vinum*, and related to Gk. *oinos*, f. which we get *oenophile*, C19th., 'lover of wine'. The word is widespread – Lithuanian, Albanian, Old Slavic have it, among others – and Eng. gets the word f. a Germanic word borrowed from the L.

Winter

OE. A Germanic word – it is present in Ger. – with an IE. root meaning 'wet'.

Wise

OE. This comes through Germanic languages (Ger. *Weise*, for example) f. an IE. root that denoted 'see' and then 'know'. Hence 'wisdom', also OE.

Witch

OE. There is a MLG. *wikken*; beyond that the origin is obscure. >wicked.

Wok

C20th. Cantonese.

Wolf

OE. A Germanic word, whence Eng. gets it. The word is present in Du. and Ger. But it's widespread in other languages like Slavic. The IE. root is visible in L. *lupus*.

Woman

OE.: the word was *wifman*; f. *wif* 'woman' – >wife and >man.

Womb

OE. a Germanic word of unknown origin. ModGer. is *Wamme*, but is only used for animals.

Wonder

OE. All the Germanic languages have it: it's *wunder* in Ger., it's *undran* in Swed. and it's *undren* in Danish. But no-one knows where it came from; which seems appropriate.

Word

OE. This goes back through Germanic languages. The root can be found in IE. source 'speak'. L. *verbum* 'word', f. which Eng. gets 'verb',

C14th., is related. 'All I know is what the words know' says Samuel Beckett's *Molloy*. The Bee Gees sang, 'Words are all I have'. And, as the first verse of St John's Gospel says, 'In the beginning was the word'.

Work

OE. This word goes back through Germanic languages, and the root can be found in IE. source which means 'do'.

World

OE. Nearly all Germanic languages all have this word, and no other branch of the family has. The root is cognate with L. *vir* 'man'. The etymological meaning of the word must have something 'age of man'.

Worm

OE., and before. This word meant 'dragon' or 'serpent' at first and comes f. Gothic *waurms*, cognate with L. *vermis* 'worm'.

Worry

OE., to mean 'strangle'; a Germanic word, and ModGer. *wurgen* = 'choke'. The modern meaning did not arise until C17th.

Worship

OE. f. *weoro*, 'worth' + *scippe* 'state or condition' as in 'friendship'. This a rare thing, a Saxon word about religion surviving. >atonement.

Write

OE. The Germanic is *writan*, and is of unknown origin. The earliest writing was done by cutting stone, and a related ModGer. word *reissen* = 'tear', 'rip'.

Wrong

OE. a Germanic word which arrived in Eng. through ON. *rangr* 'awry'.

X

Xenophobia
>phobia

X-ray
C19th. f. *X*, unknown and *Strahlen* 'beam'. The word was coined by the German chemist Wilhelm Roentgen (1845–1923).

Xylophone
C19th. f. Gk. *xylon* 'wood' and *phone* 'sound'.

Y

Yacht
C16th. f. Du. *jacht* 'hunting': abbreviation for *jachtschip*; so, a ship used for the chase.

Yang
>yin

Yahoo
C18th. In Jonathan Swift's book *Gulliver's Travels* (1726), the yahoos are a race of wild humanoid beings who are contrasted with the rational houyhnhnms who, as their name suggests, are horse-like. The word came to mean 'wild, uncouth person'. Why it was adopted for the internet search engine does not seem to have been recorded.

Yankee
C18th., orig. a New Englander, where many Dutch had settled, and prob. f. the common Du. name *Jan*.

Yashmak
C19th. f. Turkish *yasmak*.

Yarmulke
C19th. The name of the skullcap is, unsurprisingly, Yid.; its origins are in Ukranian and Polish words for 'small cap'.

Yawn
C16th. A Germanic word which goes back to an IE. root which can be seen in L. *hiare* 'gape'. It's also visible in ModGer. *gahnen*.

Year
OE. The IE. base has produced many Germanic words such as German *Jahr* and the Eng. word. It is also present in Gk. *horos* 'year'.

Yeast
OE. An IE. base means 'foam'. The Gk. word *zein* 'boil' produced Eng. 'eczema', as well as many Germanic words, including this one.

Yellow

OE. The IE. root behind this word is present in many Germanic languages (Du. *gel*, for example) as well as Gk. *khloos* and L. *helvus*. 'Yolk', also OE., comes f. the same source.

Yin and Yang

C20th. (prob.) These two complementary principles in Chinese philosophy, the first denoting the feminine, the second the masculine, are Chinese words for 'dark' and 'bright'.

Yesterday

OE. Fr. *hier* is like the first part, and the two words, as well as many others, come f. a IE. source which also produced Ger. *Gestern* as well as early Eng. *yester*. This word is a venerable tautology: 'day' adds nothing to the meaning.

Yeti

C20th. Tibetan.

Yiddish

C19th. f. Germ. *Judisch* 'Jewish'.

Yob

C20th. This is an example of backslang: the order of the letters has simply been reversed.

Yoga

C19th. Hindi, f. Sanskr. *yoga* 'union'.

Yoghurt

C17th. f. Turkish.

Yolk

>yellow

Young

OE., This is an ancient word and went into Germanic, from whence it arrived in Eng. It is in Sanskr. and L. (*juvenis* 'young'). It is there in Irish *og* and in many other places.

Z

Zany

C16th. 'buffoon on the stage trying to imitate the clown'; prob. f. It. *zanni*, a Venetian form of the name *Gianni*, which was, in turn, a pet form of the name *Giovanni* (our John).

Zebra

C16th. prob. of Congolese origin, through Port. or It.

Zeppelin

C19th. f. the name of the Ger. builder Count Ferdinand von Zeppelin.

Zero

C17th. Arab., like so many of our mathematical terms. It was orig. *sifr*, f. which we get 'cipher'.

Zigzag

C18th. f. Ger. *Zickzack*.

Zip

C19th. of imit. origin.

Zodiac

C14th. f. Gk. *zoidion* 'carved figure of a little animal'.

Zombie

C19th. f. West African *zumbi* 'fetish'.

Zoo

C19th. f. Gk. *zoion* 'animal'. 'Zoology' is earlier, C17th., and f. the same root.

Appendices

1

The Names of the days

They are all of Ger. or Scand. origin except Saturday.

Monday is 'moon's day'.
Tuesday is named after the god of war and the sky, Tiu.
Wednesday is named after the god Woden or Odin.
Thursday is named after the god Thor (compare our word 'thunder').
Friday is named after Frigg, the Scandinavian goddess of married life.
Saturday is 'Saturn's day', from the Latin god.
Sunday is 'Sun's day'.

2

The names of the months

All these are from the L. except April.

January. Janus was a Roman god who faced both ways – backwards into the old year, forward into the new. He gave his name to this month.
February is from the L. for 'purification'.
March is from the god of war, Mars. Compare our 'martial'.
April. This one is uncertain, but probably from 'Aphrodite', the Greek goddess of love.
May is from the goddess Maia.
June is from the name of the Roman goddess Juno.
July is named after Julius Caesar.
August is named after Caesar Augustus.
September is from the L. for 'seven'. The Roman year originally began in March.

October is from the L., borrowed f. Gk., for 'eight'.
November is from the L. for 'nine'.
December is from the L. for 'ten'.

3

The names of the planets
Mercury is the name of the Roman god of travel.
Venus is the name of the Roman goddess of beauty.
Earth is from a Germanic source.
Mars is the name of the Roman god of war.
Jupiter is the name of the Roman king of the gods.
Saturn is the name of Roman god of agriculture.
Uranus is the name of the old Greek king of the gods.
Neptune is the name of the Roman god of the sea.
Pluto (now demoted to 'dwarf planet') is the name of the Roman god
of the underworld.

4

Some L. and Gk. words with common beginnings (prefixes) and endings (suffixes) will help anyone with an interest in words. Here is a short list with examples. Many are listed under words in my book, but some are not:

Anti-	against	anti-clerical
Ante-	before	antenatal
Com- or co-	with	communicate
Con-	against	conflict
De-	out of	defenestrate
Demi-	half	demijohn
Dis-	reversal, lack, removal	disapproval
Duo-	two	duologue
Graph- or -graph	writing (or other recording)	graphology
Kilo	1000	kilogram
Kine-	movement	kinesthetic
Meta-	beyond	metaphysics
Peri-	around	perimeter
Poly-	many	polygon
Sub-	under	submarine

Some (but not too many) technical terms

Back-formation

A word formed from a longer word. Here are three examples: 'edit' comes from 'editor' (the latter came first); 'sculpt', which came later than 'sculpture'; and 'literacy' which is a back-formation from 'illiteracy'. Other back-formations: 'burgle' (1872) from 'burglar' (C15th.); 'lech' (1911) from 'lecherous' (C14th.). See Fowler (1996) for many more.

Calque

A loan translation: a phrase that has been borrowed wholesale from another language, and then translated. For example, English has 'man of letters', which is a version of the Fr. *homme des lettres*. Others are 'that goes without saying', also from the Fr. *cela va sans dire*, and the Irish and Sc. *usquebaugh* ('whisk[e]y') which is a calque f. L. *aqua vita* 'water of life'. 'Calque' comes f. Fr. 'trace', *calquer*.

Cognate

A word descended from the same root as another. I think of such words as cousins. For example, Ger. *Nachbar* and Du. *nabuur* are cognate with the Eng. word 'neighbour'. If they are cousins, their granddad is probably the ON *nabui*.

Folk etymology

A derivation that sounds fitting and neat, but which is false. Mr Cooper's story about 'sincere', for example, seems to have been one. More certainly, 'butterfly' does not come from 'flutter by'. The 'condom' wasn't the invention of a Dr Condom. Thomas Crapper didn't invent the flushing toilet. NEWS is nothing to do with 'north, east, west, south'. The 'Jerusalem artichoke' is nothing to do with Jerusalem, and is, furthermore, not an artichoke. 'Marmalade', and this is one of the prettiest examples, does not come from the cry of Mary Queen of Scots servants, 'Ma'am est malade'. And my brother, who was at the same London grammar school as I, has just told me that the Geography teacher told him that 'Putney' comes from the fact that the place was 'put nigh' Fulham. Oh, if only: another folk etymology.

Isolate

A language that has no relationship to surrounding languages. Finnish, Hungarian and Estonian relate to each other, but not to their neighbours; but Basque is a true isolate.

A List of Books Used – with Notes

I have included the publisher's name only when it is not obvious from the title.

John Ayto, *Bloomsbury Dictionary of Word Origins*★ (1990)
This is a beautifully written book, with entries that manage to be scholarly and yet written like concise short stories. A basic tool for anyone interested in this subject. So are other books I've asterisked.

John Ayto and John Simpson, *The Oxford Dictionary of Modern Slang* (1992)
This an excellent reference book for chasing up modern words not in the mainstream.

Robert K Barnhart (ed.), *Chambers Dictionary of Etymology*★ (1988)
The basic book. As with Ayto (above) this book manages to make its entries good stories. It is, as far as I can judge, more or less exhaustive.

Owen Barfield, *History in English Words* (1953), Faber
My interest in the history of words began when I was a schoolboy, but it was intensified many years ago when I read this book. Now long in the tooth, it nevertheless supplies a vivid glimpse of the life of the Indo-European speakers through the lens of the words they used which we have inherited, and traces the development of the language through the history of invasions.

Bill Bryson, *Mother Tongue* (1990), Penguin
What you would expect from this writer: entertaining and occasionally surprising.

The Chambers Dictionary (2003)

Collins English Dictionary (2006)★
There is little point in dictionaries that are not etymological except for quick referrals for spelling and definition. And there is not much point then, because you can get spelling and definitions from etymological dictionaries. This is a basic book, with entertaining asides throughout of word stories and folk etymologies.
   Other Collins books that I have used include their series of dictionaries between two languages: their Spanish-English, their Latin-English, and their

German-English, to take three examples. The same is true of the Oxford set of such dictionaries.

The following books by David Crystal:

The Cambridge Encyclopedia of the English Language★ (1995)
This covers many aspects of language that have not been my concern here: grammar, syntax and the sound system. All clear and beautifully written and (important, this, and not common) beautifully designed. It is impressive in its way of drawing illustrations about language from a wide spectrum of sources: entertainment, the arts, cartoon, newspapers, historical documents, jokes. The Etymology section serves as in introduction to the subject in about an hour's reading. It is very strong on the etymology of names, which I haven't been able to cover.

The Fight for English: How Language Pundits Ate, Shot and Left (2006), Oxford
A valuable and pointed riposte to pedants, best-selling or not.

Words on Words: Quotations about Language and Languages (with Hilary Crystal) (2003), Penguin
Like other dictionaries of quotations, you can spend time with this book, and find sooner or later that your time was not wasted at all, but spent creatively. Only in parts to do with etymology, it is a treasure store that sends you scurrying to other treasure stores.

Encyclopaedia Britannica
See the entry under 'Languages of the World' in Volume 22 of the fifteenth edition (pp. 600ff. for 'Indo-European Languages') for an immaculate summary of the development of the IE. family. Ignore the fact that the map still contains Czechoslovakia and Yugoslavia, neither of which exists anymore.

Jonathon Green, *Words Apart: The Language of Prejudice* (1996)
An interesting back alley of words used mostly against people.

M J Harper, *The History of Britain: The Shocking Truth about the English Language* (2007)
A denial, though by no means a refutation, of the accepted model of language development. Harper's assertions include: Anglo-Saxon is not a precursor of English; *Beowulf* is a C16th. forgery; Ireland was always English-speaking; the original Rom. Language is not L.; L. was 'a shorthand compiled by Italian speakers'. Useful for the potted history of the conventional view near the beginning.

Paul Hellweg, *The Wordsworth Book of Intriguing Words* (2003)
Any book by a man who enjoys words as much as Hellweg must be useful, and I have drawn on his -phobia and -cide words shamelessly.

Henry Hitchings, *Dr Johnson's Dictionary: The Extraordinary Story of the Book that Defined the World* (2005), John Murray

Henry Hitchings, *The Secret Life of Words: How English became English*★ (2008), John Murray
This very recent book tells a similar story to others (Barfield, for example) but is bracingly up-to-date and very readable.

T F Hoad, *Concise Oxford Dictionary of English Etymology*★ (1986)
Not browseable, but this book is an essential tool. It packs the information in a way that a more discursive book like Ayto can't.

Geoffrey Hughes, *Swearing: A Social History of Foul Language, Oaths and Profanity in English* (1998)
This book is a back alley off the main road of etymology. The contrast between its subject and its scholarly tone is consistently entertaining and informative.

The Illustrated Bible Dictionary (1980), Inter-Varsity Press
An approachable, elegant book for digging deeper into words from the Hebrew tradition.

Iseabail Macleod and Terry Freedman, *The Wordsworth Dictionary of First Names* (1995)

John H McWhorter, *The Power of Babel: A Natural History of Language* (2002), Heinemann

Eric Partridge, *A Dictionary of Traditional First Names* (1992), Wordsworth
There is a little tributary of mainstream etymology in the names we give our children, and these books are good companions for anyone interested in names in particular and words in general. 'Sophia' is 'wisdom' in Gk.; 'Ryan' 'minor king' in Irish; 'Rachel' is 'sheep', and 'Leah' 'cow', in Heb.

Simeon Potter, *Our Language* (1950), Penguin
Like Barfield, this book has been around a long time, but it still has insights that can serve us today.

The Oxford Names Companion (2002)
This the definitive reference book on a fascinating subset of etymology, covering given names, surnames and place names. To be shelved alongside Macleod and Terry, and Partridge (see above).

Shorter Oxford English Dictionary ★ (1973)
This is the two-volume version, not the massive Oxford Dictionary, and my edition is the third, not the latest; so it is occasionally shown up by later books.

Webster's Third New International Dictionary★ (1986)
This is a unique dictionary. It is fuller than the *SOED*, and has many features that will fascinate those interested in words, including line drawings of some of the nouns defined, and a huge list of English words and their equivalents in seven European languages. My only complaint is that it is possible to spend hours with it, especially the third volume, when one should be doing something more obviously work, like taking the rubbish out, nursing the baby, or solving the *Guardian* crossword. This (the highest compliment I know for a reference book) is also applicable to David Crystal's *Cambridge Encyclopedia* (see above).

CPSIA information can be obtained
at www.ICGtesting.com
Printed in the USA
LVHW021236011222
734350LV00002B/276